George from Jindivick

From Small Town Farmer to Big Cheese

George from Jindivick

From Small Town Farmer to Big Cheese

Vickie Janson

Connor Court Publishing

Published in 2019 by Connor Court Publishing

Copyright © Vickie Janson

All rights reserved. No part of this book may be reproduced or transmitted in any form or by any means, electronic or mechanical, including photocopying, recording or by any information storage and retrieval system, without prior permission in writing from the publisher.

Connor Court Publishing Pty Ltd
PO Box 7257
Redland Bay QLD 4165
sales@connorcourt.com
www.connorcourt.com

Phone 0497 900 685

ISBN: 9781925826319 (Paperback)
      9781925826371 (Hardback)

Cover design Maria Giordano

Printed in Australia

Front Cover Photos: *George at 80 on his restored Bulldozer.*

dedicated to Young Australians failing their way to success

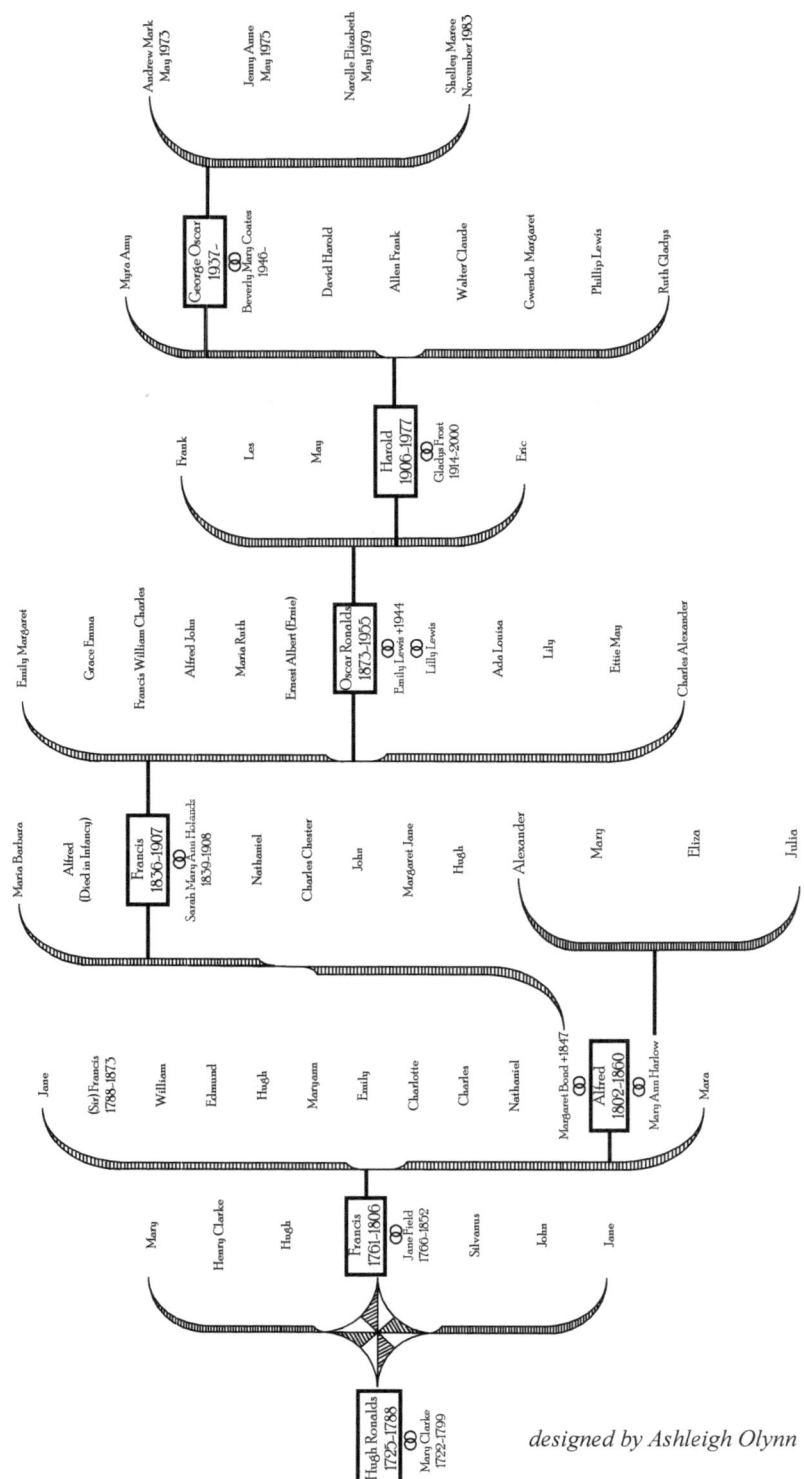

designed by Ashleigh Olynn

Contents

Prologue
The man inspired by two great earthmovers   11

1 Champion Stock   15
Jindivick & the Making of Champions   15
The Australian branch of the Ronalds family: the legacy   18
Sir Francis Ronalds (1788-1873)   20

2 The Jindivick Farmer: No job too big   27
Back in the day when … 27
Working life begins in earnest   33
Making Hay   36
Risk and Responsibility   39
Clearing the land   42
An explosive opportunity   46
The farmer takes a wife   49

3 The Jindi Story   61
Alwyn said "if I was a young fella today, I would milk cows and make cheese" 61
The prayerful and pragmatic man: Getting on with the job 63
Getting the right mix   68
Bitter Sweet   69
A legacy of hard work and innovation   70
Just a normal day making cheese   71
Having a crack at the big cheese   74
Free enough to make life fun   77
Andrew gets the experience of a lifetime   78
From Jindivick to Wisconsin   80

"We don't sell to supermarkets" 83
Topping it off with Blue 88
Dipping into yet another market 88
The end of an era 90
The farmer plants the seed … 93

4 Black Saturday: George, the Bushfires and the Battlers 95
Black Saturday in Jindivick 96

5 Beyond 1959: Warragul YFC & Australia's Spiritual Revolution 105
Farmers, Fencers & Youth Leaders 107
The Mud Bowl 112
'When discipline was fun you had a good camp' 117

6 The Blokes, the Bush, the Bravado 125
2017-2018 A Golden Quinquagenarian Age 125
Reflections of a once in lifetime adventure: Crossing the Simpson Desert 132

7 Another Pioneering Partnership 141
The Greatest Identity Forging Decision 146

Epilogue: A Summary by George 149

Foreword

Rough roads and unforgiving tracks were cherished as a learning curve for George Ronalds. Each inspiration, each journey, each mountain to overcome, were counted as blessings to be released in the pursuit of excellence.

This very human story of persistence in the face of problems, of determination in the face of defeat and laughter through difficult times, will keep you turning the page.

George and Beverley Ronalds have been on a road few travel - adventure through hope, faith and triumph. That one man would be blessed with such inspiration that takes this loving partnership from the brink of destruction to the world stage, is a rollicking story that will inspire and surprise.

Through this book you will not miss the love, the friendship and the passion of George from Jindivick in their purest form.

George Ronalds may have moved mountains of soil in his day but the seeds he planted in others will bear fruit to the generations.

-- Russell Broadbent MHR, Federal Member for McMillan

George and Bev receiving the World Championship Award, Wisconsin, 2002

Prologue
The man inspired by two great earth-movers

This is the story of George Oscar Ronalds, the boy born, raised and still living in the little town of Jindivick in West Gippsland, Victoria. It's the story of an ordinary Australian lad who began his working life clearing, farming and developing land in the region his grandfather settled in 1895.

George was a young man inspired by earthmoving equipment and he spent hours upon his bulldozer breaking up and transforming the landscape around him. To be sure, George's life is characterized by the breaking of new ground. His mechanical aptitude, practical skills, determination and sheer faith, the Australian sort that just 'has a go,' enabled this earthmover from Jindivick to break into the completely unknown business of cheese making.

In the 1980s, like many other Australians, George didn't actually know what 'brie and camembert' were. But George wasn't daunted by the prospect of making these unknown European style cheeses. He just believed Australians would get a taste for something new. The rest is history for the man who became locally known as 'Mr Jindi'.

Jindi Cheese became a world champion finessing soft mould cheeses; a dairy product previously unknown to its founder who pragmatically maintains you just "go and get the recipe and follow it". That's a recipe that outperformed the then French masters of the industry on the world stage.

George is still a living legend and inspiration to many of the current and former employees of Jindi Cheese and credits his own personal and professional inspiration to the great American earthmover Robert Gilmour Le Tourneau. Le Tourneau wasn't just recognized for the physical mountains he moved. As a devoted Christian and generous philanthropist, his contemporaries also referred to Le Tourneau as 'God's businessman'. While George and Le Tourneau shared a passion for earthmoving equipment and innovation, they also shared something much deeper; a passion and belief in another great earthmover. They shared faith in the person of Christ who could move both heaven and earth in order to transform the lives of ordinary people like themselves.

As a Four-Wheel-Drive enthusiast and all round action man, George has inspired many young Australians to have a go, take a risk and get skilled up for life's journey. As an Aussie bloke, George really breaks the mould. He is mechanically minded, earthly minded, practical and spiritual. As a dedicated husband, father and grandfather, George has poured himself into the life of his own family and broader community. For 26 years, he dedicated himself to making faith both real and fun for multitudes of young Victorians as the Director of Warragul Youth for Christ (WYFC).

George Oscar Ronalds may have been an ordinary lad from Jindivick, but I discovered he's also a national treasure.

I invite you to turn a page with me in the life of an ordinary, yet extraordinary Australian inspired by two great earthmovers who, like George, found no contradiction in living life to the full in tune with both heaven and earth. In his uniquely Australian way, George's life reflects a living partnership of skill and spirit that really breaks the mould.

George and Bev 1967

The famous ski pyramid behind 'Jindi' (the boat) 1964

George at 1 yr old in front of the picket fence that permanently bent his nose

Temporary home for 6 weeks while building their first house

Building their first home which they lived in for 41 years

George's 1975 GT Falcon, his pride and joy for 25years

The old Chev after they decided it needed to be a ute

The old Chev 50 years later

George's with his grandchildren on his self-restored Chev, 2017

1
Champion Stock

The name Jindivick is of Aboriginal origin meaning 'Burst Asunder' and appears to have been named soon after 1873 when Drenegott Hubner had his block surveyed. The area was named during the surveying of the Melbourne to Sale Road. An assistant surveyor named Upchat was moving camp by packhorse when a case of surveying instruments insecurely fastened by an Aboriginal horse boy fell from the packhorse and burst open. Fearing punishment, the boy fled into the scrub. Upchat seized him for a moment and demanded to know where he was going. The boy shook himself free and ran off shouting 'Jindivick, Jindivick.' Upchat asked another Aborigine what Jindivick meant and several weeks later when the surveying party had to name the area where the Aboriginal boy had disappeared, Jindivick seemed an appropriate name.[1]

Jindivick & the Making of Champions

Jindivick, West Gippsland is a modest town 12kms north of Warragul and is home to approximately 600 people. This includes four generations of the Ronalds clan. For those requiring a bigger landmark, Jindivick is about 110 km east of Melbourne, Victoria.

---

[1] A condensed extract from *Burst Asunder; The First Hundred Years* written to commemorate the Centenary of the Jindivick Primary School 1877-1977.

According to Bunce's *Language of the Aborigines of the Colony of Victoria* (1859), Jindivick is an Aboriginal word meaning 'burst asunder' and significantly 'Jindivik' was the name given to the first pilotless rocket ever developed with its first-time flight in Australia in 1952. Maybe it's something in the soil, for despite its size, Jindivick has produced several high-flying champions who have burst out of the region disrupting the status quo.

One of those champions landing amongst the stars was Lionel Rose from Jacksons Track Aboriginal community. Jindivick was the only place of settlement the track passed through. Rose's burst of fame came in 1968 when he won the title 'World Bantamweight Boxing Champion'. Being the first indigenous Australian to win a world title and the first indigenous citizen to be named Australian of the Year, put both Rose and the Jindivick region on the world map.

In 1996, it was back on the map again with the founder of Jindi Cheese, George from Jindivick, being catapulted from this far-flung corner of the world to Wisconsin, USA to accept the award for 'World Champion Soft Mould Cheese'. This would be just the beginning of the Jindi Cheese championship era. Whether it really was something in the Jindivick soil or just a legacy of sheer perseverance these champions inherited, history affirms there was certainly something in the Ronald's DNA that continued to produce winners.

George's grandpa Oscar was the first of the Ronalds clan to settle in the district and become a Jindivick champion. Born in Ballarat, Oscar then ventured off to Western Australia for a stint with the Perth Railways. In 1895, he was drawn back to Victoria to take up farming in Jindivick. His brother Ernie also bought into the district.

Following the Land Settlement Act of 1869 the government were selling blocks of land up to 320 acres at one pound per acre, on terms of two shillings per acre for the first year. The first Jindivick land sale was made in 1878 and in 1895 Oscar selected part of Charlie Masons selection, ending up with a considerable amount of property, which he and his sons developed into choice farmland. It was on this land that Oscar produced his champion daffodils. He had a particular burst in notoriety when he famously created the first pink daffodil. In 1900, Oscar selected a further 500 acres down Old Telegraph Rd at the bargain price of 10 shillings per acre, sold to him on the condition that he would fence it. And this he did. But the 'first's' attributed to Oscar weren't restricted to his pink daffodils. Oscar's 1915 T-Model Ford was also the first car in the Jindivick district causing quite a bit of excitement. The old Ford car rallies are still a cause of excitement to many Australians. When 150 T-Model Ford enthusiasts from around the world spilled in wonderful procession into Jindivick in 2016, it was clear they still provide delight to the locals.

This said, Grandpa Oscar's fame really was riding on his daffodils. In a comprehensive Ronalds family history published in 1985, compiler A.F. Ronalds noted the horticultural journals were still acknowledging him as one of the greatest daffodil breeders who ever lived. This clearly wasn't just a family bias. Having scooped up the 1950 Royal Horticultural Society of Australia award for the best yellow trumpet, bi-color trumpet and pink daffodil, the *Melbourne Weekly Times* acknowledged Oscar as the 'well-known daffodil authority.' In 1969, fourteen years after his death, the Australia Daffodil Society established the Oscar Ronalds Perpetual Trophy to commemorate his achievements.

Oscar's son Harold also inherited a horticultural hand. The year before Harold married he purchased a dairy farm of 150 acres of land opposite his dad's farm and to supplement his income, he successfully grew peas. Perseverance and adaptability, as farmers know, are critical in producing the good seed, stock and breeding for champion produce. When the Ronalds DNA is put under the telescope of time, there is much more than champion daffodils and pea harvests that come into focus. As if written into their DNA, perseverance and adaptability can be observed to have spanned across more than four generations over 200 years producing a legacy of champions.

The Australian branch of the Ronalds family: The Legacy

It was Alfred Ronalds, George's great, great grandfather, who established the Australian branch of the Ronalds family migrating from Staffordshire, England with six of his children in February 1849. He sailed on the 'Lord Hungerford'. Alfred and Margaret's first born son had died in infancy and perhaps this is why Alfred chose to leave his youngest infant son Hugh in the care of relatives in England. Tragically, Alfred's wife also died just two months after Hugh's birth and so Alfred arrived in Australia as a widower with the six other children. When they first landed Maria, the eldest of Alfred's children, was sixteen and her closest sibling Francis was twelve.

Travelling across treacherous seas to an unknown land with six children would be daunting for most. But Alfred, with an eye for opportunity even from afar, was not deterred by these circumstances. His eye remained on opportunity and he arrived in 1849 equipped with all the apparatus ready to set up his engraving and printing business. He also spotted another opportunity on the long voyage to Australia in the person of fellow traveler Mary Ann Harlow. They later married adding another 4 children to the existing family.

It was a very different world in 1849. When the Ronalds clan arrived in Melbourne the population was only 17,000 and Victorian infrastructure was in its infancy. At this time records affirm there was 'no vehicular track to Gippsland'. Perhaps this is why Alfred decided on arrival to turn westwards and settle his family in the more developed region of Geelong. The State of Victoria was still part of the colony of New South Wales but change was in the wind. Alfred saw the historical significance of Victorian statehood as well as the business opportunity this presented. Credited as the earliest copper-plate engraver and printer in Victoria, Alfred designed a 2-inch diameter commemorative medal to be 'Commemorative of the Great Charter of Self Government Granted to the Colony of Victoria.' (5 August 1850) This medal was not government sponsored but Alfred's private venture; another enterprising endeavor for which the family was renowned. Not only would the Ronalds family go on to win championship medals, the very first Ronalds business entrepreneur in Australia crafted an historically significant one.

Necessity often breeds enterprise and Alfred certainly came from a household that necessitated enterprise. He was the eleventh of twelve children where sibling survival skills would no doubt have been in play, particularly after his mother Jane was widowed with seven children under thirteen when Alfred was only four. There is no doubt his mother must have been very enterprising. All the children received a good education. It was the type of education that unlocked the innovation and excellence already planted within their DNA.

While little is known of Alfred's father, Francis Ronalds Senior (1761-1806), it was recorded in 1799 that he was a cheesemonger in London and a competent businessman. This is quite ironic given that in the distant future his great, great, great grandson George would also get a taste for the cheese industry in the far-flung settlement of Jindivick on the other side of the world. Like his ancestor, George would become a competent businessman establishing Jindi Cheese whose produce would return to be sold by English cheesemongers and appreciated by European palates.

Sir Francis Ronalds (1788-1873)

The most famous historical member of the Ronalds family was Alfred's elder brother Sir Francis Ronalds (1788-1873). He was sixteen years Alfred's senior and it was Francis who sparked Alfred's interest in electrical experiments. Francis left school at only fifteen with history recording he possessed 'a little taste for physics and a smattering of geometry'. His achievements with that 'little taste' were remarkable. Whatever shortfalls there may have been, his education can be credited with cultivating and expanding the inquisitive and productive mind Sir Francis possessed.

Like many others in the Ronalds family, Sir Francis was described as a thoroughly pragmatic man with 'little interest in the classics.' He loved to experiment and he set up a small studio especially for chemical experiments. Due to his consequent fame, the road where it stood was renamed Ronalds Road to commemorate the location of those initial experiments. In 1813, with electricity becoming the new science, Sir Francis moved from here to fit out a large hay loft for his electrical experiments. Young Alfred, the father of the Australian branch of the family, assisted him in this.

In 1816, Sir Francis invented the first telegraph. A.F. Ronalds notes in the family history he 'proved its practical application by sending messages instantaneously through eight miles of aerial wire rigged on a wooden framework and then through 525 feet of glass insulated wire in wooden troughs lined with pitch and buried four feet deep, all in the garden of his house at Hammersmith'.

Having made significant contributions to the invention of the telegraph, I imagine if Sir Francis could have jumped in a time machine to visit the 20th Century, he'd not only be amazed at the ingenuity of pragmatic George, his great, great, great nephew, but probably find it comical that this distant relative should set up business near Ronalds Hill, on Jindivick's Old Telegraph Road, tapping into something of a legacy.

When you consider the descendants of the Ronalds family, you have to wonder if ingenuity and some inventive gene with a proclivity to embark on big projects isn't embedded in their DNA. Albert Francis Ronalds, the son of Ernest (an older brother to George's grandfather Oscar) was the first chief civil engineer on the largest engineering project in Australian history; the Snowy River Scheme. He was also the Chief Engineer on the Upper Yarra Dam, and as Engineer-in-Chief of the Melbourne Metropolitan Board of Works (MMBW) 1955-1967, Albert oversaw the construction of the Gippsland to Melbourne gas pipeline that initiated natural gas distribution in Australia. The same type of attributes appear to have been activated in Albert's daughter Professor Beverley Ronalds. Beverley credits her father as the inspiration for her own pursuit of a civil engineering career and was not deterred by being the sole female student in her class in the late 70s. With characteristic Ronalds' humility, Beverley recognizes her father's achievements noting that he won the Argus Scholarship, 'which I was fortunate enough to win 46 years later'. In 2011, Professor Beverley Ronalds, Group Executive, Energy CSIRO, was listed among Australia's Top 100 most Influential engineers.

Like his famous distant uncle Sir Francis, George loved to experiment and enjoyed investing time in simply figuring out how to make things work. His own homegrown inventions transformed many ordinary farm and household implements into practical business tools. While they may have shared a curious and pragmatic mind, a love of life, a sense of humour and possess that 'have a go' spirit, one notable trait George and his famous relative didn't share was a love of books. George simply wasn't a reader and he and his wife would later confess they were always too busy working with their hands to read. George would go so far as to say that reading was often considered a waste of time by those working the land. This sentiment would stand in stark contrast to the view of Sir Francis who was an avid science book collector and author. He was an academic who had many published works beyond those relating to his electrical inventions; one of the more notable being 'Mechanical Perspective' which was published in 1828. This was a printed description, or guidebook, of the devices in his self-built semi-automated production facility produced to assist his customers in their use. Several hundred of his machines were sold as a result of 'Mechanical Perspective'. Although George may not have invested the same time in reading, he was naturally pre-disposed to understanding mechanics with what seemed to be an inherited ability to put that understanding into practical use. Perseverance and adaptability continued to outwork through the generations ensuring the Ronalds family continued to produce champions. In 1844, that 'little taste for physics and a smattering of geometry' resulted in George's great, great, great uncle Sir Francis being elected a 'Fellow of the Royal Society' for his eminent discoveries in electricity and meteorology; the highest distinction a British scientist can be awarded by fellow scientists. A century and half later with faith that Australians would get a taste for a new European cheese, George would receive the highest distinction among the world's best cheesemakers. They had different tastes and different lives but were both bred from the same champion stock.

The achievements and skills of George's four times removed uncle were exceptional and yet the same perseverance and adaptability were evident in his younger brother Alfred; George's twice removed grandfather. The commemorative medal Alfred had designed and produced offered him distinction as an engraver yet Alfred didn't rest on former achievements. He continued to pursue new opportunities and in 1851 joined the Victorian gold rush. His capable hand produced detailed drawings of a gold-washing machine for inclusion in a treatise 'Patent Washing Machine for Economising Labour' by Ure and Herbert. The gold rush took Alfred and his family to the Ballarat region where in 1854 he adapted himself once more, investing both money and energy into market gardening. This love of horticulture, together with the seeds of perseverance and adaptability, were subsequently instilled into his son Oscar and grandson Harold enabling them to fall on Gippsland soil where George would be born.

Alfred, the father of the Australian branch of the Ronalds family was notably versatile. Like his father before him and descendants to follow, Alfred was a competent businessman. He was a competent draftsman, engraver, copper-plate printer and lithographer. He also undertook survey work and finally became a prize-winning horticulturalist. At the March 1860 Ballarat Horticultural Society Show, the fruit of Alfred Ronalds life was displayed in his prizewinning grapes (three varieties), peaches, cucumbers, apples (two varieties), pumpkins, marrow, celery, red beet, leeks, peas, brans and parsley. The most notable fruit of his life, for which he received public acclaim at its end, was an outstanding harvest of perseverance.

In a comprehensive and lengthy obituary only a month after the horticultural show, *The Miner and Weekly Star* noted "The deceased gentleman possessed considerable and varied talent, combined with indomitable perseverance." That's a strain of perseverance that can't be subdued or defeated. It's the type of seed that breeds champions and given that, it's probably no surprise that his great, great grandson George might inherit a desire to be one. While the word 'champion' sounds terribly romantic there is nothing terribly romantic about 'indomitable perseverance.' Yet this is the trait that often enables champions to be born as they fail their way to success.

George and his brother David proved to be no exception. They always wanted to be the champion spud producers; the local 'Kings of Potatoes'. But blight attacked their initial crop bursting that particular aspirational bubble. They then turned their attention to pumpkins but drought ensured that crop also failed. Eventually, they decided to take their father's advice and try their hand with peas. As George would say, "these were the days when you listened to dad". Their father Harold had enough previous success with peas and having made some money from them, "this seemed like a good plan." Whether or not their dad's peas were 'champion peas' may not be recorded but standing on two generations of horticultural success, George and brother Dave continued to invest their hope and energy in that Jindivick soil for a marketable crop.

George recalls taking that first load of peas to the Melbourne market and setting up his stall next to Wally Kenney. This positioning must have been of a prophetic nature. George and Wally would remain side by side throughout their lives in friendship, hardship, faith, work, family and leisure. George and Wally would become inseparable. It was fitting that fellow horticulturalist Wally should be by his side on this first opportunity for George to reap the rewards of his own horticultural endeavors. However, when George opened that first bag of peas it was clear his horticultural career had been brought to an abrupt end. Alas, the peas were all mouldy. The Jindivick champion breeding ground beckoned him to try something else; but that would be getting ahead of the story.

George proudly standing on top of some of the removed 1500 stumps

Moving Oscar Ronalds house by Bullock Car

Snigging logs in 1959

Going to school on the Milk Truck 1948

Nitropril at work

Burning windrows

George's scrapers 1980's

Jindi cheese now stands middle right of photo

Reconstructing a dam 1983

Grandfather Oscar Ronalds T-Model Ford, the first car in Jindivick

2
The Jindivick Farmer: no job too big

Back in the day when …

George will tell you those were the days when there was "no dole, no super and you could blow things up!" Gelignite and farming went hand in hand. In this small rural community into which George Ronalds was born 16 November 1937, innovation wasn't a luxury but a necessity.

Bigger families were the norm and they tended not to stray too far from home. George's family was no exception. He was the second eldest of 8 children and George still resides today only 500m from where he was born. This is the same place the pre-schooler got stuck under the picket fence and had his nose broken as he was being pulled out. To this day, a slightly crooked nose reminds him of the event.

With an early fascination for how things worked and loads of places to explore and things to experiment with, young George was known to get himself into a bit of mischief. Very long hot summer days had to be filled providing 5-year-old George and his 4-year-old brother Dave plenty of opportunity. One such day they came across the old draft horse who had backed into the air space in the milking shed to cool off. Like many youngsters, they were fascinated by fire and very curious as to whether the horses tail was flammable. So, they decided to experiment. The first few attempts at throwing a match towards the old horse's tail didn't reap any real results but to their delight, their perseverance eventually paid off. The old draft horse suddenly took off like a rocket. As it was a very short-lived thrill, the lads made the overall assessment that their experiment was most dissatisfying. No doubt the horse would agree. The poor creature's tail was reduced to a stub within 10 quick seconds and that was all it took for the boys to realise a horse without a tail is not something you can hide from your dad. Being an era where the strap provided a useful lesson in cause and effect, young George and Dave had their own experience with a hot tail later that day!

Although George would only ever move 5kms from his birthplace, some very big moves are part of the family history. From their beautifully manicured home today, George can point to "just behind those trees" where he was brought up in his father's house. And looking in the opposite direction, he looks down upon his grandpa Oscar's old house which was transported from one paddock to another by bullock cart to make one house out of two. That literally takes moving house to another level.

The Jindivick State School 5kms up the road was attended by George, his siblings, his father and uncles, and some of the extended Ronalds family still attend today. The school has its own story of some of the big moves needed to overcome the environmental hardships of rural life. You could say moving mountains, houses and even schools was once pretty much the norm in Jindivick with no job too big for those early pioneers.

The first school was erected in 1876 in what is now Quarry Rd.

This was a portable school carted from Melbourne; a journey of approximately 70 miles or 110 km. One of the contractors noted "the nine miles from Drouin Junction to Jindivick was about one of the worst roads in Gippsland" and a 'tongue in cheek' article about the state of the roads in the district published some 70 years later suggests it took quite a while for them to be upgraded.

> Up to this stage I had assumed that the 'bursting asunder' referred to some pre-historic volcanic upheaval, but now found it referred to some modern cataclysm that had befallen the roads of the district. One could not travel 100 yards without encountering a broken spring or bolt or tail light or other relic of a vehicle which had passed before ... We travelled over most of the roads of Jindivick during my tour and perhaps that is why I can say but little about the hinterland but one glorious scene will forever remain imprinted on my mind and that was while my guide was replacing a back wheel which had shaken off and run into the blackberries on the North Rd and I could look over Starvation Flats in comfort.[2]

Given this 1947 account, it's difficult to comprehend the state of the roads in the 1870's and the herculean task of moving a house or a school. What we do know is tall trees and deep mud dominated the lives of Jindivick residents in the 1870-80s when the school was first moved to the district. This was also just prior to the time George's grandfather Oscar settled there.

The 1947 *Gippsland Independent* goes on to highlight the continuing local mud problem and the need for a good pair of gumboots claiming "The average depth of mud in the cowyards in winter is 19 ¾ inches." The issue is documented more seriously in Shire minutes of the period which register complaints about animals smothered in mud and their legs broken on bridges resulting in no other way for farmers to get their produce to the Melbourne market. Somehow

---

[2] *Gippsland Independent*, 14 August 1947.

these pioneers must have found ways, because as early as 1890 this was a prosperous farming district.

While the early transportation of the Jindivick school was successful, the schoolyard remained a muddy morass and there was understandable concern about the portable buildings which were renown for being short on nails and bracing. This gave them a bad reputation for wriggling in any sort of wind. It clearly wasn't ideal to have such a flimsy school positioned in a small clearing which was over-shadowed by 300 foot Blackbutts; those majestic trees that produce wonderful designer hardwood floors today. A strong wind in any direction could result in falling trees capable of crushing the school and, it should go without saying, all the precious students within. Understandably, concerned parents and residents began to petition the government for another school move. With the road from the old site to the new being described as "something fearful at this time of year," the school on Quarry Rd was nevertheless demolished, transported to Jackson's Track and rebuilt on the new ground in June 1881. It then had to be defended against the 1898 bushfires. Having worked so hard to get it on site, nobody was willing to let it go. Despite some damage to school and its defenders, the school was saved. With consequent growth to the area, it was refurnished and officially re-opened in October 1909 where it still operates today. George's dad Harold, and all the Ronalds family to follow, attended this same embattled school.

The 5km round-trip, which would otherwise be a substantial daily walk, was alleviated somewhat by a visit from the milkman. The milk truck would call into the farm to pick up cans of fresh milk around 8:15am enabling George and siblings to jump on board the back of the truck to get to school. The long walk home in all weather conditions remained part of the normal school day routine until Harold invested in a girl's bicycle, enabling George to dinky home with his brother.

The year 1943 was historic for the Jindivick State school not only because George started school, but because in November the school purchased a battery-operated wireless, better known today as a radio. As progressive as this may have been, progress in other areas was quite slow. Some Jindivick residents enjoyed electricity as early as 1938 however the primary school wasn't connected to power until 1951. This meant George didn't benefit from that particular luxury as he graduated to secondary school in 1950. He completed Form 3 Junior High Certificate at Warragul High School with the 'Warragul High School Speech Night' on Thursday 11 December 1952 acting as a rite of passage. The program can still be found in George's old briefcase of special treasures and reveals a lot about Australian culture and the musical influences shaping the lives of these Gippsland youth. The evening commenced with 'Songs by the School' and sandwiched between the National Anthem and Beethoven's Creation Hymn was 'The Seekers' by Sir George Dyson.

'The Seekers' that first spring to most minds are the 1960s pop quartet; fellow Victorians Judith, Athol, Keith and Bruce who were jointly named Australians of the Year in 1967. Like many other performers, these Seekers started out as a folk and gospel group shaped by many of the same cultural influences as Warragul High School students graduating in 1952 with George. But it wasn't those Seekers on the program. It was a composition called 'The Seekers' by Sir George Dyson which was chosen for the auspicious occasion of the Warragul High School Speech Night. Dyson's biographer Paul Spicer provides a revealing analysis of 'The Seekers' which provide insights into the prevailing norms:

> The Seekers ... is a stirring and singable tune in the unison song tradition of the period. As always it was written entirely, practically with adolescent boys in mind and the range restrictions of their voices. The song lies mainly around a low C-G area rising to E flat to the climax of each verse to which Dyson leads the voices very naturally by step. The theme of aspiration in the text is also important to notice...it encourages the young man to develop his independence, to aspire to the unattainable and to have a 'burning hope' which lights his path of life. It is very much in the ethos of the English public school of the period. Dyson's tune has a masculine vigour entirely fit for purpose.[3]

Spicer's analysis of The Seeker's makes a rather explosive statement in today's cultural milieu yet Principal at that time, P.F. Wilkin, reported to the *Warragul Gazette* "the students were heard in a splendid musical program".

It is the 'theme of aspiration' that is particularly significant and the embodiment of these aspirations in young men like George who indeed were independent; who did aspire to the unattainable and did have a burning hope lighting their path. These sentiments couldn't be more fitting for this 15-year-old's graduation and his entry into adult life.

Being the second week of December, Speech Night also included carols. These were followed by the School Song and many formal presentations including the Citizenship Cup and Citizenship Prizes gifted by the Shire President reflecting an appreciation for citizenship somewhat absent from contemporary education.

It seems as if so much more was once achieved in those limited school years. George and his wife Bev will tell you they worked very

---

[3] Extract: *Sir George Dyson: His Life and Music* by Paul Spicer The Boydell Press, Woodbridge 2014 page 130

hard at school but they never had any homework. That's probably just as well with all the home chores allocated to kids living on farms. But those hours at school reaped some exceptional results equipping young people for employment and life more broadly.

As a grand finale to the evening, the 16 top achievers across Forms 1-6 in the school received their awards. George was awarded the Form 3c DUX Prize with his Report Book noting George was "a fine lad…a neat worker with excellent results … a keen and most helpful pupil both in literary and practical subjects … taking full advantage of the benefits of school in every way." The form teacher simply concluded that George had "completed an excellent year". That's leaving school on a high and certainly a report card you can take home to mum and dad with confidence. George would continue to take full advantage of the benefits afforded to him in every other aspect of life. He was born to look out for new opportunities.

Working life begins in earnest

As was quite common in those days, George left school to enter the workforce when he was only 15 years old. Things were different then. At 15, the Ronalds' boys were allowed to buy their own gun and there were plenty of rabbits and foxes to pursue. They would 'go bush' with Dad and Uncle Eric for some Roo shooting. George recalls the great excitement the first time he shot a Roo and rather than associate winter time with a change in weather, George associates it with fox hunting. He loved all the outdoor adventures, especially trout fishing in the local streams but Lakes Entrance was his favourite spot. Joining your dad in the workforce at 15 was less daunting when you're already carrying your own gun.

As a farmer's son, working, not just long walks, had always been part of his ordinary life experience. Milking the cows occurred twice a day and like most other farmers, this started between 5-6am. George recalls the rough concrete in the cow shed and the holding yards outside being mainly dirt and mud. They were gradually concreted but there was no ready-mix concrete. This meant the cement had to mixed with a shovel making it both slow and heavy work. And as pressure pumps were still a future innovation, the shed was cleaned by strong arms and backs hoisting buckets of water.

George's dad Harold had a standard 'walk through' dairy shed and farmed before the days of refrigeration. From the shed the milk went to the milk room where it was cooled through a single plate cooler to approximately 20 degrees. It was stored in 45 litre milk cans that stood alongside the shed to be collected by the milk truck that had transported George to school.

Harold's dairy shed was set up to milk four cows at a time. With up to 125 cows, which was a fairly large herd in those days, this made for quite a long day. It normally took George and Dave about 2.5 hours to milk those cows. Sundays were not exempt but being raised in a Christian home, the day offered a change of routine.

After milking on Sunday morning, the whole family would attend the 11am church service and the kids went on to the 2:30pm Sunday school service in the Rokeby Hall. Rokeby, being a small saw milling town, only offered one little shop and a small church however, the hall could cater to the 70 or so lively kids that turned up for Sunday school each week. It was his dad who introduced George to youth work. Investing in youth was somewhat of a Ronalds legacy. George's grandfather Oscar was one of the founders of the Rokeby Union Church and he started the first Sunday school in the district. 30 years on with a couple of moves, this initiative was still operating having been handed to his son Harold and later to Wally, George's younger brother.

Harold and George's uncle Eric taught Sunday school from 1930 until the 1970s. In the same family tradition, George at 15 not only took on work commitments but became a local Sunday School teacher at Rokeby Hall and like his predecessors, he occupied this role for the next thirty years. It would be hard to imagine entrusting the lives of dozens of younger children to a 15-year-old today. But it worked well then.

What still amazes George today is that 90% of the kids who attended the Sunday school came from homes where their parents didn't go to church. These were the days when non-churched parents thought church was still a good thing for their kids; a very positive influence. Church wasn't just viewed as a place to cultivate faith, but to cultivate values, a sense of identity, community, culture, social skills and a place to learn history and traditions. It was also where many met their future spouse.

In those days, George and a team of others would go out each Sunday morning to knock on doors and round up all the kids wanting to be transported in cars to Sunday school. This was an era when parents trusted that children were in a safe place and in good hands with their neighbors at the local church. Every year the parents packed out the Rokeby Hall, about 150 of them, for the Sunday school anniversary presentation. These parents, who otherwise never heard a church message, were delighted to watch their kids sing and recite biblical verses. Christianity, and the values it imparted, were a vital part of Australian culture and social life even for the unchurched.

While George was passionately involved in Christian events, his passions were never limited. To quote a school project authored by his daughter Narelle, 'Dad's important event was when they invented the tractors around the 1950's. That was a big event for dad since he lived on a farm." (In Narelle's mind, tractors were just invented: what could possibly be older than the 1950's!)

He was sixteen and working the farm with his dad when George got his first taste of tractors. Until this time, horses were used to do all the heavy work and George became familiar with their limitations. The equipment towed behind the laboring horse was not very efficient and so it was good news for all, including the horse, when his father Harold purchased a tractor in 1953. Tractors were still rare on farms at this time and Harold was the second of two farmers in the district to have one. This not only made life easier for George and the horse, but sparked within him a greater interest in mechanics.

Making Hay

According to the online resource the 'Grammarist' the expression 'make hay' has a few definitions. First, it's short for the proverb 'make hay while the sun shines'. Hay is difficult to prepare in wet weather, so the proverb points to the wisdom of taking advantage of opportunities while they're available. Second, make hay means to turn [something] to one's advantage. This newer sense derives from the first one, perhaps originally out of confusion over the meaning of the metaphor, and it involves making hay out of something specified. In the first sense, what the hay is made of isn't relevant.[4]

George was a man who made hay both metaphorically and literally and tractors revolutionized the process. They were used in conjunction with the stationary hay press which would sit in the middle of a paddock. After the hay was windrowed, the tractor would push the hay up to the baler. For the urban folk, a windrow is a long line of raked material, in this case referring to hay. But it wasn't just an easy day riding on the tractor. The hay then had to be forked into the press and the knots on the bales tied by hand. George said "it was a frightful thing to work." In time, New Holland recognized how impractical this was and later the Pickup Baler was developed, which made it a lot less frightful.

This was a great era of innovation and the master of innovation who ultimately fanned into flame George's passion for earth-moving equipment was Robert Gilmour Le Tourneau. In the 1950-60's Le Tourneau was producing earth-moving equipment 3-4 times the size of contemporary equipment. This wasn't because it was the mechanical dinosaur age. George maintains it was the sheer size of the jobs in those days that demanded these enormous machines. "The biggest scraper at that time could move 360 yards of dirt. By comparison, the biggest one today moves about 50-60 yards. The roads can't transport machines that big anymore." Le Tourneau had a great influence upon George and what a creative mind could achieve with an understanding of mechanics. George recalls Le Tourneau in the 1960's predicting that cars would eventually have electric motors. It was Le Tourneau's books and his success as an

---

[4] "Make hay", grammarist.com.

innovator, businessman, and Christian philanthropist that inspired George to keep persevering and complete those extremely 'big' jobs. His books still stand in George's office.

The Burst Asunder publication compiled by the Jindivick Centenary Committee offers some historical context to the incredible impact on farmers of this transition from horse to tractor in the 1950s.

> Blackberries were probably winning their war with the farmer. Manpower shortages during the war had found that blackberry cutting was a task which could not be done and the bushes were 15 feet high in places and many a fence would have fallen down but for their support. Galvanised iron and pipe were available after a long delay or if you knew someone who knew someone. Suddenly things changed. The catalyst was the Korean war which forced butter fat prices so high that for the only time in memory the dairy farmer was ahead of the rest of the community in economic terms. Farmers supplied manufacturing milk at the expense of the Melbourne milk and Melbourne was short of milk for a couple of winters. In 1952 all milk for Melbourne was vested in the Milk Board and the Board issued contracts that were binding for the first time. This relative affluence was rapidly converted into capital investment on farms and at the same time very conveniently the Ferguson tractor and hydraulic system became available. Think of practically any machine which uses the hydraulic linkage of the tractor and you have a development of the 50s.[5]

The publication also notes that as electricity supply increased in the district, farmers began to weld, drill and grind metal in jobs that had once been only a tradesman's preserve. Power to the farms enabled farmers to literally become 'a jack of all trades'. George's life certainly testifies to that. His love for mechanics wasn't limited to farm machinery and in 1955 George (17) and Dave (16) purchased their first car: a 1928 Chevrolet. This would be the beginning of a

---

[5] Jindivick Centenary Committee, *Burst Asunder: Jindivick - the first hundred years*, Warragul, The Warragul Gazette, 1977, 46.

collection of 'boy's toys' which would ultimately require a shed the size of an aircraft hangar to house. Today that shed stands next to George's home with a sign over the door; 'Pa's Shed.'

Pa's Shed displays many of George's toys including the Jindi Fire truck, three Go Carts, 1941 Jeep and a lifetime of tools. But in pride of place is his first car, that beloved 1928 Chev. It may be a little rusty but is still very functional. To the delight of three generations of the Ronalds family, it's motor will still turn over with a powerful roar. In his 80th year George completed the timber backend tray so the grandchildren could be taxied around the property. What was once an everyday ride and fun experience for all in the 1950s is now quite a novelty. With no seats or seat-belts and lots of bumps providing a taste of freedom and adventure for George's grandchildren, this might even be considered a little risqué by some. Grandchildren of all ages experience great delight in the Old Chev.

Risk and Responsibility

Since boyhood George's life has been characterized by an uncanny ability to shoulder big risk and big responsibility. It was obviously a big deal to purchase his first car as an 18-year-old in 1955, but it was an even bigger deal for an 18-year-old to jointly purchase 500 acres of bushland from grandpa's estate with his 17-year-old brother and set out to clear it. That's what these brothers did. They bought a rather large bush block considered not suitable for farming having been told it was "Kangaroo Country with second rate dirt." The availability of fertiliser in the early 1960's would alter that prognosis and 50 years later the number of stock per acre (or hectare) was about the same as other land being farmed in the Jindivick region. However, the depth of topsoil increase today is staggering; from 5cm to a whooping 400cm.

Fertiliser was certainly a game changer. When George and Dave started clearing in 1958 the fertiliser was transported by steam train from Geelong to Rokeby Rail Station. It was packed in 180 pound bags (90kg). Anyone who might have picked up an overweight suitcase, something over 25kg, will appreciate that a 90kg bag of fertiliser is heavy! The brothers loaded the heavy fertiliser on to their old Ford truck for the 6km trip to the farm where more hard work awaited them. After reloading it onto the farm trailer behind the tractor, the fertiliser was ready to be spread. One lucky person had the job of driving the tractor while the other stood on the trailer tipping the heavy bags of fertiliser onto that 'second rate dirt'. It was hard rough work. In late 1958 the railroad closed and the fertiliser began coming directly by road. Not too many more years later, bulk bins were introduced. This made life considerably easier for these farmers.

George and Dave's Old Telegraph Road bush block was named Old Telegraph Rd because it was the route of the first telegraph line from Melbourne to Sale. The Melbourne stage coach travelled Old Telegraph Road for a few years but one wonders how. The brothers discovered the road was almost impossible to get through in winter so it was fortunate the fertiliser was delivered in February. Once the men started clearing the land they did a little work on the road as well to make it passable all year round.

When Grandpa Oscar first selected the bush block on Old Telegraph Road, he milked on his home property and used this bush block as his haystack in winter. That's because there wasn't any hay baling at that time. Farmers would burn off patches on the farm in the summer, drive the cows out to the bush to winter them, and bring them back to milk. In 1955 when Oscar died leaving the 500 acres to three of his sons, one of them being George's dad, this gave George and Dave the opportunity to buy it. The going price for the Old Telegraph Road bush block was 7 pound 10 shillings an acre. The brothers borrowed this at 4.5% from their uncles and in 1957 began clearing it on a part-time basis. With George venturing into dairy farming and Dave into beef, completing the task would take them 10 long years. The brothers also helped their Uncle Les, an A Class builder from Warragul, build a home on a block adjacent to the Belgrave Heights Convention site. The building was originally built for youth camps but today Myra, the eldest of George's 7 siblings, resides here. And Myra still accommodates families attending the convention site. George attributes much of his building skill and knowledge to this experience with Uncle Les.

Before they started clearing the land in 1958, George and Dave were busy splitting posts, and shooting foxes and kangaroos on the property. Fishing also offered an occasional escape and pleasant indulgence. It was post-splitting that can be attributed to George and Wally Kenney's paths first crossing. Having witnessed George's attempt at producing prize peas, Wally could more authentically admire his post-splitting endeavours. This friendship would go much deeper than 'peas and posts' and their sense of humour no doubt made some good fun of the analogy. Wally loved fencing as much as George loved dozers so when he heard Wally and Dave were post-splitting it was a natural marriage. They all admired strength and tackled big jobs and in this district, Wally was really famous for his big fence posts. A normal fence post would be about 150mm in diameter but Wally's were always 200-300mm. George says Wally's corner posts were 'really something special' and they had to use the bulldozer to load them on the truck. George relays a story about Wally's corner posts with the sort of excitement and delight you expect when someone has witnessed something truly beautiful.

> We had an old Ford army truck and Wally would have a corner post that would be about half a metre wide - I'm not exaggerating, it would be at least 7-foot-long - and when I'd take it home there was no way of holding it to get it off the back of the truck so it had to be dropped in place. There was no way of lifting it so about 6 of us would 'up end' it on the truck and there'd be this almighty thump and you'd feel the vibration when it hit the bottom of the hole.
>
> Then it took about half a kilometre of wire to go around the post before you could start a fence that big. We used to go and find a big tree and you'd cut it into lengths and that was the start of Wally's fence. By the time you finished the fence it was almost waterproof. The wires you used to put on them you know … the rain wouldn't get a hope of getting through it! Those fences will still be standing in another hundred years…so that's how I got to know Wally through the fencing business.

And their friendship remains as strong as those fences.

Clearing the land

The bush continued to dominate the landscape all through the 1950's and there simply wasn't enough land for people to farm in the district. Clearing it became essential. Hiring other contractors to do the job on their own block was going to be incredibly expensive so in 1958 George and Dave decided to buy the machinery and do it themselves. They purchased an Allis Chalmers HD9 bulldozer for 4,250 pounds. It had the 471 GM motor which George says was the Rolls Royce motor of the day. "The motor was music to the ears when running and came complete with tree pusher." In George's eyes, it was "glorious!" Despite having spent 25,000+ hours on it clearing bush and building dams, the dozer is still going today. Now fully restored, it's in a collection of bulldozers at Peter Cuthbertson's quarry opposite the farm in Old Telegraph Road. The collection includes his beloved HD11 Allis Chalmers which George bought sometime later.

All in all, this was a period of incredible growth for George who was now 21 and preparing to transform the landscape into something that resembled hospitable farmland. That meant tackling enormous trees, hostile scrub, and blackberries that even Goliath could shelter under. There was nothing but bush and bog from West Jindivick Road to Labertouche. About 400 metres from West Jindivick Road on Old Telegraph Road, a Coudaroy crossing had been constructed over Mosquito Creek. Urbanites could be forgiven for not knowing what a Coudaroy crossing is! It's a crossing constructed with saplings cut from the bush and laid side by side perpendicular to the road to provide a path over the boggy ground.

The bush had not been logged for many years and was a naturally hostile environment. Despite this, these young entrepreneurs could see the potential in the valuable timber standing on the land. George could see the potential in not just clearing his own land, but pursuing contract work in the district and he now had the equipment to do the job. With their two other brothers looking after the home milking, opportunity presented itself and in 1960 George, Dave and the dozer turned to contracting. In the colloquial there was 'heaps of work' clearing land and building dams. And they didn't have to travel far to work only ever venturing 20-30km from home. The brothers engaged Alan Aitken and his son Ian to log ahead of them and the log royalties provided much needed income. The down side was the thousands of stumps that remained making the clearing more difficult. It wasn't all about tearing things down. Utilizing the poles cut from the bush and some second hand galvanized iron, they also built a big shed on the block. The starting post for the shed was actually a tree, still rooted in the ground and cut to 4 metres high. This was a living shed. Little did they know this humble shed would stand for 45 years to be replaced on that same spot by the Jindi Engineering Workshop; an adjunct to a yet to be conceived World Champion Cheese Factory.

Thousands of acres of land were cleared and settled in the district in the 1960's and the scale of the jobs was daunting. George will tell you there's very few people who know about land clearing now and that's mainly because they've passed away. There may be a number of reasons recruiting for the task today would be difficult but George is convinced the main obstacle would be the sheer work involved through all seasons and conditions. Sitting on those old open dozers all through the cold winters and very hot summers; the hours, the labor, the dust, the dirt and the numb bum may not meet contemporary expectations.

Clearing was seasonal and winter was the season to push the trees over. This was because the ground was soft enabling the roots to be dislodged more easily. A tree pusher was attached to the dozer to push the trees over in a row, i.e. into windrows, where they would remain for up to 12 months to dry out before being burned. When they were burning off, George would be on the bulldozer from 6am until well into the night. It was as exciting as it was strategic burning those windrows.

Fire restrictions were lifted in autumn and the right day to burn off was a coolish one with a gentle breeze when the windrows were tinder dry. The idea was to start the fire quickly by running alongside the windrows with a lit branch allowing burning leaves to drop. The large fires made their own atmosphere and lowered the humidity resulting in a fire even more fierce. Despite the intense heat, George loved to watch the big ones. That boyhood fascination with fire was satisfied by 50-100 acres or more of burning windrows, the flames leaping 50-60 feet into the air. Once the atmosphere cooled down a little, the dozer was cranked up and the burning logs were pushed together into heaps stoking the fire. After the windrows had been pushed apart and re-heaped they would burn for a few days. George recalls working by feel because the dust and ash was so thick he couldn't even see his dozer let alone the windrows the dozer was manipulating apart. The burn off could take several weeks.

It was dirty work and hard on the machinery. Hours were spent servicing the dozers with particular attention given to the air cleaner. And it wasn't just the dozer that got dirty. While a strong canopy on the dozer protected George from falling trees, there was no cabin so by lunch time he was completely black from the soot. On the positive side, this thick layer of dust and soot offered George full protection from the sun; there was no need for sunscreen. But there was a need for a good shower so George made his own in the living shed he and Dave had constructed. His own instant hot water system was made from a copper tank over a gas burner enabling George to come home reasonably clean. He still applauds his mother for washing his filthy clothes and cutting his lunch.

Winter was the time for repairing equipment and constructing things and a cut off 12-gallon drum used as a fireplace warmed the workshop. The dozer tracks required a lot of maintenance and weeks were spent welding worn out parts. But by the early 1970's, it became more efficient to buy new rather than repair old ones. George's mechanical mind was not just born out of necessity, mechanics was a passion. And just as well, as the motors in the old tractors often needed repair. His father also found amusement on a small International Crawler Tractor and most days would visit the workshop in his short wheel base Land Rover. George recalls both his father and those vehicles fondly.

An explosive opportunity

Not all the trees were a push over job. Clearing also involved using a lot of explosives to rip the tree stumps out and 'gelignite George' was up for the task. (Actually, it was Dave). The sawmill would often go ahead of George and Dave and cut the trees off at the stump to about a metre high. This was to prevent marking or damaging the trees to be milled. The logs would then be carted off to the mills nearby leaving "horrible stumps." Then the gelignite boys were sent in to blow them out. Local opinion was that Dave was very good at it hence his nickname 'Powder Monkey.' After drilling about a metre under the tree, Dave dropped 2-3 plugs of gelignite under the stump. This would either split it or lift it enabling George on the dozer to push it over in bits, leaving a lot of mess. Many weeks were spent picking up sticks by hand that were left behind and piling them up ready for a bonfire. It was all very labor intensive.

Outside commonsense, official safety regulations for the use of explosives were somewhat unheard of and there weren't any licenses for contractors to undertake this sort of work. As George confesses, "we just learnt how to do it by doing it." How to discern a safe distance from an explosion was based on experience. "You might walk 10 yards away from the stump when blowing it up but that would depend upon how much you put under it." Having blown out an astonishing 1500 stumps on just one of their own 50 acre paddocks and retained their limbs, it was assumed their experience was reliable. The only permit required was for the explosives themselves and this was obtained from the local Warragul Police who were familiar with their work.

Not all of George and Dave's safety experience with explosives was something to crow about. Their Uncle Les had a farm nearby and as the story goes, had asked the boys to blow the heavy concrete top on a well next to the dairy because he wanted the well filled. Having been advised 2-3 sticks of gelignite covered with clay would blow down, they decided to give it a go. They positioned the explosives and lit the fuse, and then retreated to a safe distance. As they watched, a rooster, apparently fascinated with the burning fuse, came around the corner of the shed. This was no ordinary rooster. He was one of the prize roosters on the property belonging to the share farmer, John Roxby. Captivated with curiosity and cocking his head from side to side, the prize rooster followed the wisp of smoke along the fuse. By now John was frantically waving and yelling in an attempt to divert the rooster's attention but it was to no avail. That fuse was much more fascinating than the antics of any crazed man. An enormous bang then launched feathers and rooster into the air depositing him about 15 metres away. With most of his feathers plucked, he staggered a few more steps before expiring. Despite the rooster becoming unintended collateral damage, their mission for Uncle Les was accomplished. But it certainly wouldn't be something to crow about to the share farmer!

By 1963 George had cleared enough of that Old Telegraph Road bush block his grandfather used as a haystack to build a dairy there. At 26 he built a whole new dairy; the walk through shed, bales and all that was required. There was no electricity so the milking machine was powered by a diesel motor. George would travel from the home he was raised in to the dairy twice a day with the first visit around 5am for the morning milking. He says he *only* milked 80-90 cows at that time because throughout the day he was either clearing or contracting. That same year he'd purchased 80 acres at Rokeby to clear and develop. After a day of either clearing, baling or building dams, George would be back at the dairy by 5-5:30pm for a couple of hours to milk the cows again before heading home. In his own words "we were young and energetic and that's just what we did." George's first year's milking income was £2,240.

Despite the intense workload, George always found time for recreation and never neglected his spiritual life. The same year he built the dairy he was appointed to the Warragul YFC (Youth for Christ) organizing committee and later became the Warragul Director. As an expression of his faith, George dedicated many years to building life skills, confidence and resilience in the districts youth. He also ensured they had a lot of fun and built these attributes into his own family life. In 1962 George and his brother Alan picked up their first ski-boat somewhat prophetically naming it *Jindi*. It was quickly hotted up with a more powerful motor and water skiing became the recreational activity for the entire Ronalds family. Water skiing would captivate all 5 brothers, 3 sisters, and be something 2 more generations of the clan would later enjoy to varying degrees. George's friend David Rowse also had a boat so they would often go to Lake Narracan near Yallourn on a Saturday or after the evening milking. George was always having a go at new things and seemed to be attracted to risk. After seeing professionals demonstrating the pyramid at the Moomba Ski Show, George and David decided to have a go themselves. Skiing behind Alan, who was steering *Jindi*, the innovators used a broom handle to keep the distance between them. They then had Vic Wallace stand on their shoulders. While they did eventually master the exercise, getting to that stage offered onlookers spectacular entertainment as they repeatedly fell off. George taught a lot of people to ski throughout his life and at 80 years of age, is still driving the boat for his youngest pupils; the grandchildren.

The farmer takes a wife

The 1960s were a time of great change. Not only did power come to George's house in 1965, cars were becoming more reliable and more people had them. This resulted in the need for better roads and the 60's saw many large highways constructed and other roads upgraded. The distance between people became shorter and the opportunities greater. So too for George.

A young Melbourne lady, Beverley Mary Coates, was frequently on those roads to visit her aunt, uncle and grandmother who lived in the Jindivick district. As fate would have it, they attended the same church as George's family and Bev became good friends with his younger sister Gwenda. Gwenda often went to Melbourne to stay with Bev and the families lives became intertwined.

George describes their relationship as "a friendship that just grew" and recalls their first 'pinky' with fondness. They were on the way back from a YFC snow trip and there was a 'dug out' in the side of a hill, i.e. a snow cave for sheltering and warming by a fire. A few of the travelers went in to check it out and among them were Bev and George. It was here their little fingers crossed for the first time and their hearts began to intersect.

Consequently, George started making more regular trips to

Melbourne which he describes as "quick trips." This was probably because he was still a young man with a full life and he needed to be home by 11pm to keep up the workload. George says "there's nothing like a quick trip" and this was the general sentiment of an age whose legacy was a very high road toll.

In the 1960's, road safety consciousness was yet to emerge and attempting to do 'the ton' - i.e. 100mph (miles per hour) – wasn't uncommon. 100mph is about 160kph (kilometers per hour) which really is a quick trip. Speed was a habitual killer. While authorities today strive to keep the local road toll under 200, Bev can recall the days when it reached 1200.

When George was courting Bev he had a self-imposed 11pm deadline to be back home. Travelling around 70mph (that's 112kph) he would normally only have to dip his lights once or twice all the way. Apart from the less than perfect roads and possibility of roaming wildlife, there were no seat belts, heaters, coolers or demister's. Hitting fog was common and George explains how you'd have to have one eye actually out the window. Those cars fitted with a strip demister offered the driver the advantage of keeping both eyes in the car while peering through the demisted strip of window rather than physically stretching to keep an eye out the window. Understandably, these trips kept George's guardian angels very busy.

Given that George was a rural farmer and Bev worked in the bustling city of Melbourne in a merchandising office, it may have been difficult to see what they had in common. Bev's employer was Dowd's, a lingerie manufacturer, which offered her a working environment in stark contrast to farm life. Ironically, Bev had spent her whole life telling people she would never marry a farmer. She hated farming, was scared of chooks and never did milk a cow. However, Bev did learn to work the dogs, round them in and confesses she didn't really mind cleaning the shed. At risk of sounding stereotypical, the truth is that Bev enjoyed home crafts like knitting and sewing. On the other hand, George was totally an outdoor man who simply loved sitting on his dozer, was keen on sports and loved water skiing, 4WD'ing and generally those things considered exhilarating by risk takers. Despite these obvious differences, George and Bev have enjoyed 50 years of marriage working through countless difficulties and adventures together. Something that sparked in that 'dug out' in the 1960's contained enough substance to fire up a commitment to a new life together that hasn't only 'done the distance' but enjoyed the steps along the way.

There is a saying, perhaps better known in past generations, 'families who pray together, stay together.' It may have been this spiritual dimension to their shared life that played the vital role in their marriage, mitigating any natural differences. Their compatible personalities and shared sense of humor were an added bonus. And their shared character traits not only made them attractive to each other, but to others. While excelling in different physical domains; Bev predominately inside the home and George out, they shared a commitment to excellence in many areas. Both Bev and George were incredibly hard workers who were willing to get their hands dirty but kept their hearts clean. They creatively made and mended things from sheds and motors to jumpers and meals. Both were very hospitable, practical, laughed a lot and maintained an optimistic outlook. Both were incredibly humble. George and Bev were, and remain, doers rather than spectators of life, modelling for others what sacrificial service really looks like. Being so like-minded and united in heart, it becomes less surprising that after commuting to Melbourne for two years, rural George and urban Bev decided to marry.

That change in circumstances meant George would need to get a home on the family block and the first step was to approach the bank manager, as only George really could. When asked when he wanted to start building George replied "I already have!" And then George proceeded with a rhetorical question to illustrate who was keeping the nation afloat …

> Have you ever really worked it out … there's not really very many of us running this country. Do you realize 48% of people work for the government and none of them earn any money they just use money that we provide for them…out of the other 52% most of them work for somebody else in private enterprise … that wipes most of them out of running the country. About 5% of people are self-employed who are really running the country. You're only there because you survive on the interest I pay you. If people like me weren't around, you wouldn't be there either. There's only really about 2-3% of us that are really running the country.'

When relaying the story, George concluded gleefully, "I got me money."

And he also got his bride.

On the 17 June 1967 Beverly Mary Coates married George Oscar Ronalds at Bon Beach Gospel Chapel in Victoria. Bev loved Queensland and with that in mind, they spent their honeymoon in Surfers Paradise. Their new £13,500 home wasn't quite ready in time so George and Bev's temporary marital home was an old caravan near the cow shed.

George continued milking and clearing land, and that same year as a newlywed he started contracting in earnest. For this purpose, he purchased a New Holland Pickup Baler and Rake. In the summer when it was time to harvest George would be cutting, mowing and baling hay. In the same year he married, he also purchased a Land Rover IIA and commenced 4WD bush trips which would become a hallmark of George's life. Everything just got bigger and the excitement for life never dulled.

George also maintained his role as Sunday School teacher and was appointed an elder of Rokeby Church in 1968. Because of their continued involvement in YFC and weekly church life, Bev became one of the first people in the district to have a dishwasher. Doing the dishes had become quite a chore with all the guest speakers at the Ronalds home for dinner and George disappearing afterwards to milk the cows and drop people off. This meant Bev was left with the lot. Understanding there's nothing like a happy wife for a happy life, George remedied that with this rather progressive addition to the home.

To George and Bev's delight, after six years of marriage they had a son. Andrew Mark Ronalds arrived 31 May 1973 relieving Bev from the sickness that had accompanied her entire pregnancy, not just in the mornings but all day. At this time, the demands of all the contract work meant George was having difficulty keeping up with the home milking and he decided it was all becoming too much. It was time to shut down the dairy, sell the herd, just run some beef on the home farm and stick to full time contracting. This is what he did.

Both the business and the family were in a growth phase. Within two years Jenny Anne Ronalds was added to the family. Jenny was born 2 May 1975, followed by Narelle Elizabeth Ronalds 10 May 1979. There were gaps between the children as Bev plucked up the courage to face the prolonged period of sickness that plagued her pregnancies. Their fourth and final child, Shelley Maree Ronalds was the only one not born in the month of May but like the others, she was born at the Warragul hospital. Shelley arrived 11 November 1983.

George was present to see all their children born which was unusual in those days, even for farmers. When the doctor spotted tears rolling down George's face at the births, he became concerned for his welfare. But these were tears of wonderment and joy. George says it's something he will never forget. Bev was glad he was there but jokes about the limitations of his involvement. George will tell you he lost his license for nappy changing early in the piece after the first one fell off and his attempt at washing nappies was to put them on the clothes line and get the hose!

One thing the entire Ronalds family did do together and do well, was holidays. They always had family time out and the last week in January was always spent in the caravan Bev's parents had bought. The rule was they could use it as long as they towed it where Bev's mum and dad wanted; which was Lakes Entrance. It would be towed to Lakes Entrance just after Christmas and remain there until March or April. But the big weekend was always the last one in January when David and Lois Rowse and their kids joined them.

There would be water skiing, fishing and lots of shared time and activity. While the kids didn't develop George's love for fishing, they did enjoy skiing with Narelle aspiring to be as good a skier as older siblings Andrew and Jenny. At only 8 years old, Shelley was on a single ski. According to Bev, when they were growing up the girls were more naturally adventurous and more likely to just 'have a go' than Andrew who was more captivated by computer technology. Yet this too was turned to adventure with Andrew later gaining his pilot's license. Jenny didn't have any interest in computers but excelled on the piano and this led her to pursue a career as a music teacher. The children may have all had different passions but they were raised in an environment that encouraged active pursuit of these whether it was work or play.

George was always passionate about his work and his beloved machinery. This was just as well because as he confessed "at the end of the day you virtually end up working for your machinery." George found it wasn't much of an asset because by the time he'd paid it off, the machinery was worn out and needed replacing. But he continued to contract because it did give the family a living and he had a lot of fun along the way.

Much more significant than the lifespan of George's machinery was the end of his dad's life. On the 7 August 1977, after reading his last words to the Rokeby church congregation, Harold Lewis Ronalds suffered a massive heart attack. Breaking every speed limit, George raced him to the hospital in his Falcon GT. But it was too late and Harold passed away.

This same year George bought the first of two Wabco Le Tourneau electric power scrapers to tackle the big earthmoving jobs. A lot of the bigger irrigation dams in the area that extended from Sale to Frankston were George's handiwork. He had a reputation for tackling the big jobs others couldn't manage with his dam construction being somewhat celebrated. Sometimes George was asked to re-do dam's other contractors had constructed. Locals could always spot George's dam's because they included a signature island. Around this time, George got involved with the Soil Conservation Authorities (SCA). The SCA was a semi-Government organisation which offered very low interest loans to qualifying farmers for the construction of irrigation dams. The SCA provided an engineer to oversee dam construction, take levels, mark out the dam and conduct daily compaction and moisture tests and George worked with SCA on a considerable number of dams throughout West Gippsland. Most of these were across gullies or creeks. The construction method was similar to the way big earth compacted dams are built, such as Upper Yarra Dam where George's cousin Albert Ronalds was the Chief Engineer. All the dams had to be rolled with a sheepsfoot roller and a water cart was used to get the right moisture content. Every job offered different challenges, whether a creek running through or the need to bridge a swamp by building a 'Coffer dam.' A Coffer dam is a temporary dam constructed upstream from the main wall from where the water can be pumped around until the core trench is completed and the pipe pushed through. George gained much of his experience and expertise in the construction of dams and general earthworks working with the SCA. Yet he never limited himself to one business stream and took on other work as opportunity presented itself. He undertook a lot of road works for the Warragul Shire and also spent about 3 months a year in the neighboring Labertouche district. Here the sound of his bulldozer alerted locals to his presence in the district. As one neighbor talked to another, the work just followed.

One afternoon, George and fellow contractor Mick were travelling home on their dozers after clearing bush at Labertouche, when George spotted the Shire Foreman Sid Anderson on Old Telegraph Road. There can't have been any traffic to speak of as the men drove their dozers straight down the middle of the road.

Having a personal and professional relationship with the Shire offered George the privilege of making a few suggestions and he wasn't backward in coming forward in that regard. In his forthright, opportunist fashion, George offered Sid a couple of hours free of charge while they were there in order to knock the top off a hill he felt needed levelling. Not too much discussion was needed as Sid agreed this sounded like a good plan. How times have changed. The foreman simply put up a 'Road Closed' sign and without regard for formal protocol, that road was levelled and improved for all commuters. In this pioneering era, the cultural environment was quite different. The most often asked question was not 'why?' but simply 'why not?'

When he was hay baling, George employed John Ballantyne and introduced him to the power scraper. George and John did a lot of work together and also had a lot of fairly explosive fun. One day they were putting in a dam for a potato grower in Warragul South. At the front of the farmer's potato paddock there was a huge gum tree about four metres in diameter. George thought it was probably one of the old Strzelecki Gums, which would be protected today. The potato grower asked George if he thought he could shift that huge tree. Unsurprisingly, George said "why not?" He always wanted to know what would happen if you put a whole bag of nitropril underneath a tree and this looked like a great opportunity to find out. George hadn't used nitropril before but was keen to find out what it could actually do. He sought some advice from local quarry man Norm Mills who he knew pretty well. Norm told him nitropril was "pretty powerful stuff" and recommended what he should do with it. George proceeded to buy a 50-kilo bag of nitro-fertiliser (nitrogen fertiliser) which he was told would act in the same way as the nitropril. In those days, anybody could buy it. George carefully followed the instructions he was given and mixed it with diesel in a wheelbarrow. Using a 4inch or 100 ml post hole digger, George and John then drilled about 5-6 holes underneath that huge tree, dropped the mixture in, connected it all together and stood away further up the paddock. George remembers looking up the tree and seeing a crow sitting in it. He thought, "if I were you, I'd shift!"

George told John to light the fuse because "you can run quicker than me." So that's what John did. They were standing about 100 meters up the paddock and had no idea what to expect. The first thing they saw was like a miniature atomic bomb. A cloud rose above the tree and mushroomed over the top. The pair looked on in wonderment and the silence was golden for the first second or so. Then a great blast of air hit them – 'woof' – and nearly knocked them over. Then they heard a bang like they couldn't believe and looked up in the sky. There were great chunks of timber flying around which they had to dodge. When all the dust cleared away, the hole that was created from the explosion was big enough to bury the dozer. There were bits of tree everywhere. Later they found out the explosion was heard in Warragul (about 15kms away) and there was an old lady in the house above them they had forgotten to tell about the planned explosion. All her windows were rattling and she nearly jumped out of her skin. This was the beginning of their reputation in the district as the blokes who could deal with the trees that were too big to chop; the ones the chainsaws wouldn't have been big enough to deal with. This was one big tree! George saw the owner about 2-3 years later who told him "you know that tree you blew out … I'm still picking up rotten bits of wood in me spuds from it!"

George really enjoyed those years working with John and has fond memories of what some might call their multi-tasking 'manifold wisdom.' On-lookers observing their work would sometimes smell the pleasant aroma of slow cooking meat. Having wrapped their sausages in foil and positioned them on the heat of the scraper's manifold, the duo could have lunch prepared while they worked. But although they had a lot of good times and gained a lot of mechanical experience – experience with electric motors, taking levels in dams and different types of soils – George was aware there were no long-term prospects. His eyes remained open for the next opportunity.

George pushing the scraper on Ronalds hill

George and Mike heaping for the burn

Jindi Cheese Factory 2003

Jindi Truck

Craig Sceney stirring the curd

Three of the cheesemakers, Matthew, Craig and Shane checking the cheese

Jenny, Bev and Edna packing

Jindi's orginal packaging

3
The Jindi Story

Alwyn said "if I was a young fella today, I would milk cows and make cheese."

Andrew was now ten years old and George was still earth moving. He had a lot of work constructing dams and contracting to the shire but he could see the downturn and was looking for another opportunity. At the local Gideon meeting one night, long-time friend Alwyn Jensen, a retired farmer, asked George what he was doing. George replied 'I'm looking for another opportunity.' That confession to Alwyn would be instrumental in remoulding George's life story.

Alwyn told him "if I was a young fella today, I would milk cows and make cheese."

George was curious and as a young fella of 48 years old, he thought he better look into it. In the early 80's the only cheese Australian farmers knew about was cheddar. Alwyn had faith that Australians would get a taste for the European style cheeses. At that time, George had to ask what Alwyn meant by European style cheeses. "Brie and Camembert" said Alwyn. "What's that?" said George. They both laughed about it later.

It might seem like a bit of risk to mortgage your farm to build a cheese factory when you have no experience at all with cheese, let alone European cheeses that were virtually unknown to the Australian public. But, as a man of faith, George always believed he was led to do so and never thought this venture would fail.

Alwyn's son Laurie was involved in a fledging cheese factory in Neerim South. He had completed studies in dairy technology at Gilbert Chandler University and providentially was looking to partner with someone to make these sorts of cheeses. With George looking for an opportunity and Laurie looking for a partner it didn't take long before a great plan to build a factory and make mountains of cheese was drawn up. George and Laurie weren't complete strangers as they'd both previously been involved in Youth for Christ (YFC); George as Director and Laurie and his brothers as singers. Now they had other common ground to sing about and others began to join their choir.

One of those was his lifetime friend Wally Kenney who George relied upon as the executor of all his good ideas. George and Wally would now have the opportunity to execute all of Laurie's good ideas! Although a man of few words, Wally offered an interesting turn of phrase to describe the contrast of moving from bulldozers to blue cheese: "Pretty amazing really that George and Bev could come up with something really out of the blue like that." Out of the blue indeed. Wally himself might be also seen as a man of great contrasts. He had a cattle stud, and also an eye for beauty in strong fences and delicate flowers which he grew and sold in the Melbourne market. George's big ideas always needed Wally to execute them properly because he was a stickler for detail. If they were going to build a garden together Wally would turn up with a shovel and George with a bulldozer. One of those big ideas was to sell Jindi poo from the dairy effluent. George will tell you with a smile on his face, "that it never got off the ground." In 1984, George told Wally he was thinking about building a factory and might need a hand. That hand was never withdrawn and Wally would ultimately be working full time at Jindi Cheese. He became the full time 'rouseabout' executing all those good ideas.

Once George and Laurie's big plan to build the factory was in place, George approached the bank. At the time, interest was a hefty 18%. With the family farm on the line, George went ahead and borrowed $35K to move their dream cheese factory off Laurie's drawing board and onto the farm. Jindi Cheese was born in 1984 and henceforth was affectionately referred to simply as *Jindi*. Those few words at the Gideon meeting sparked a new hope that was about to be realized: 'If I was a young fella today, I would milk cows and make cheese." That's just what they did.

The prayerful and pragmatic man: Getting on with the job

Being the pragmatic man in the business partnership, George aided by best mate Wally, got straight on to the job. They revamped the walk-through milking shed into a Herringbone dairy. For the uninitiated, this looks a bit like the inside of a whale and enables a much larger number of cows to be milked. Then they built the new factory Laurie had designed. Brian O'Connell was employed to do all the steel work. He had an engineering shop in Trafalgar. George and Bev had met him and his wife Kathy at Lakes Entrance 12 months earlier. Both couples got on really well, as did their kids who were about the same age, and they are still in contact to this day. Brian eventually closed his own Trafalgar workshop to work full time as Jindi's fabrication engineer. He would oversee 13 extensions to the factory and all the maintenance.

With George and Bev's family home and factory on the same property, Wally took care of the aesthetics revamping the gardens and even building a fish pond. He was meticulous with the selection and placement of every rock, and some jobs required truckloads of them.

While George wasn't fazed about manufacturing a cheese he had never tasted, building a factory with little knowledge of cheesemaking did prove a challenge. George reasoned that making cheese was like making anything; "you just go and get a recipe and follow it." But back in the day it was mainly the French who held the gold standard recipes and who were making the soft mould cheeses for the world markets. France was a long way from Jindivick and George found obtaining the right information to master the finer details of cheesemaking rather difficult. These were the days of telex machines and telegrams, not mobile phones and instant communications, so it was all trial and error and the first few months proved to be disastrous. Reflecting on this, George quotes Robert Gilmour Le Tourneau, a man whose life and inventions continue to inspire George: "My experience gave me my mistakes and my mistakes gave me my experience".

And there were plenty of them! What George and Laurie discovered was that producing world class cheese is a lot like life itself. George says "it's all about what you do with it on the way." Mistakes along the way add to great stories and every good story has something major to overcome or a villain lurking in the shadows who seeks to rob and destroy. In the Jindi story that villain was *Mr Whiskers* and like all shadowy characters, he came out at night.

Mr Whiskers was the name George and Bev gave to the black mould that would infest the cheese overnight. It was the bane of productivity and an enormous test of perseverance for the fledging business and family. After leaving the factory maturing room in perfect condition each evening, Bev with infant Shelley in tow, would return in the morning to confront Mr Whiskers. Like the shadow of a man's whiskers cast over the pristine white cheeses, the 1cm overnight growth was unrelenting and seemed to be uncontrollable. The ensuing battle against bacteria relegated Bev to many days spent pulling Mr Whiskers off the precious infant cheeses. Sadly, most just couldn't be saved. The process was both gruelling and costly turning the mould room into a war room.

After throwing out the offending cheeses, the maturing room would be sterilized with a fumigation bomb designed to kill everything. This arduous task often had the Ronalds family cleaning until midnight to eradicate every trace of the villain. The room was cleaned, dried and re-seeded. The secret of the maturing room was to get it full of the same penicillin mould being used in the cheeses to encourage the growth cycle. By reseeding, i.e. spraying the penicillin mould around the room itself, the penicillin mould would fall from the room acting as a catalyst to healthy growth in the cheese.

After these sustained bacteria battles, each day became a little more demoralizing. Mr Whiskers only needed 12 hours to resurface and recast his shadow over the fresh fledgling white cheeses. The mop up and preparation was time consuming, costly, repetitive, unproductive and continued this way for months. Bev recalls her 40th birthday well because the visitations were particularly bad that September. A birthday visit from Mr Whiskers was nothing to celebrate.

With things not going so well, George lent on past problem solving methods. He found the approach he had in the earthmoving business wasn't cutting it in the cheese business: "In earthmoving, if I had a problem I would ring my competitor and talk to him. In cheese, if you asked for help, people would laugh at you."

Fortunately, George did know who he could always call on. Displayed over his desk is George's favourite Bible verse which says it all. He paraphrases this quite simply as "I called, you answered." This is a paraphrase from the book of Jeremiah 33:3 and isn't just a pleasant platitude but a living banner over every aspect of George's life. He called and he expected a practical answer to a practical problem. George was not disappointed.

Everyone considered it an answer to prayer when Laurie won a Gilbert Chandler Scholarship enabling him to go to France to learn more about cheesemaking. This was the breakthrough Jindi Cheese needed and through this it was discovered the problem wasn't with the Jindi recipe per se. The real problem was the Jindi environment. They'd built the factory in the middle of a farm.

Manufacturing cheese in the middle of a farm full of bacteria from pine trees, hay sheds, the cows, the dairy (and just about everything else on a farm) proved to be not the ideal. Laurie and George learnt that Jindi's success would depend upon them installing a specialized air filtration system to purify the air flowing into the factory. They also learnt the factory had to be pressurised to maintain a constant pressure like a hospital. Unless they could achieve these conditions, the infant cheeses were never going to make it to market.

Once they knew what had to be done, good old fashioned ingenuity and sheer will kicked in. These were not the days when farmers called in electricians, plumbers or other trades; they just figured out how to fix and build things themselves. Back in the day, a Form three education combined with hands on rural life experience could actually equip you to solve significant problems. Pragmatism and mechanical aptitude were all in the farmer's toolkit and the Jindi team drew on those skills to manufacture their own air filtration system. To their credit, it worked very well.

> "We soon realised the air filtration system was not adequate for what we wanted. What we needed was a fully controlled temperature for the manufacturing room and other areas of the factory, ranging from 23 degrees to 3 degrees for the cool room. We also had to keep a constant filtered air flow through the factory, so when an outside door was opened air flowed out not in. To achieve this, we installed positive displacement air fans sucking air through big hospital type filters and then through heat exchangers for the heating or cooling of the factory. At the opposite side of the room was a vent to let the air escape and to keep a constant pressure inside.
>
> The chilled water for cooling came from ice bank units which we made using old milk vats. We used 19ml copper tube wound around a drum to form a coil approximately 60 cm in diameter and placed the coils in the milk vats. Our refrigerator man then hooked these coils to a refrigerator unit to make our ice water which was pumped through the heat exchangers when required. The hot water for heating came from the boiler used for the pasteuriser. It was all controlled by a thermostat. The heat exchangers were off shelf units using the same principle as car radiators. These worked very well and we used the same design to build much larger units making our own tanks as the factory grew in size. They were efficient because they used cheap night rate electricity.
>
> We made a large ice bank unit to cool the milk in the dairy and using second hand Zero vats for the milk, we found after repairing them using Bars Leak they performed very well."

As a footnote, George repaired these by mixing 3-4 cans of Bars Leaks, the sealant you use to repair radiator holes with about 12 gallons of water and pumped that around the vat for about an hour. He was ecstatic to discover the vats actually sealed and were still holding water when he sold them 10 years later! Their ice machines are still working today and as a spin off from it, the much smaller enterprise, Jindi Engineering was birthed.

Getting the right mix

Both the process and the source of milk in production were equally important. Jindi's 200-head herd comprised 75% Jersey's and 25% Holstein-Friesians. Jersey milk had the highest protein and casein content of all milks on a per litre basis. It also had excellent fat solids producing a high protein cheese with an incredibly smooth and creamy taste. Initially this 'you-beaut' milk was pumped from cold storage vats through underground pipes to the plant 25 metres away. With later growth, it would arrive in milk tankers from selected local farms. The first stop for the milk was the factory lab where the butterfat was calculated and from here it flowed into the now perfectly conditioned cheese factory to be standardised. As George explained "milk can vary from different farms and what was milked on a wet cold night in the winter time is a different structure to the middle of Spring. It's different again in summer and as the cow gets later in lactation then the milk quality alters. Cheesemakers need to be on the ball to detect that and that's why we used to standardize ours."

Standardising was something that happened every day to obtain a particular butterfat depending on the product. Milk from the cow could be anything from 3.5% to 5.5% butterfat and Jindi used old fashioned methods of standardisation. They simply let the milk stand in the vat overnight and after testing it would know how much cream was on top and how much butterfat was underneath. Then they would just pump off the skim milk underneath and standardise it. But there was nothing standard about what their methods produced and with some help from Bill Studd, then of Butterfields, Jindi finally sold its first cheese into the Melbourne market in 1986. The family's prayers, team perseverance, and pragmatic problem solving had combined with quality controlled processes and high protein milk to deliver a winning recipe. Unsurprisingly, George could see a market on the horizon for Australian Soft Mould Cheeses that could really be milked.

Bitter Sweet

The sweetness of those first sales in 1986 were quickly soured the following year when George and Laurie realized they had blown the 1987 budget. The factory was only handling about a quarter of what had been forecast and with all the unbudgeted costs Jindi Cheese was 4-5 times over budget. That was a scary place to be in. George was advised he had to throw in another $200K but with the risk he was already carrying, George was determined at this time not to put in another cent. As far as George was concerned, they would either make Jindi go as it was or close it down.

Laurie suggested the crisis could be alleviated by securing an investor to buy the potential of Jindi and successfully negotiated with a large earthmoving company to buy the debt. This seemed like a good proposition and a profitable deal was worked out between the parties. But when George and Bev presented the proposition to their solicitor, he advised them against it fearing loss of the family farm to the new investor. In the end, no deal was signed.

Having overcome the serious manufacturing challenges and just six months earlier employed cheesemaker Craig Sceney, George now found himself not really knowing what to do next. He could see there was a market for his product but had enough education to do the maths and understand the current deficit.

After some inner wrestling, George and Laurie could only envisage three possible options. Either George could take over the factory, or Laurie could take it on, or a merger with another dairy company might be reached.

Having invested so much of himself in the venture and not believing it would really fail, George, being an all or nothing kind of guy, opted for a crack at 'all.' Obviously, this would require him to carry all the debt. But let's face it, he was used to carrying heavy loads and he knew who to call on when the load was too heavy. His faith and family always offered the reassurance the load wasn't entirely his to carry. George and Laurie's partnership was dissolved and the Ronalds family, facing the prospect of a large financial loss, took on Jindi Cheese lock, stock and barrel.

A legacy of hard work and innovation

The factory itself was a testament to rural ingenuity and innovation. When George needed to lift his elderly mum into the truck cab for a bit of a spin around the farm, the forklift provided the ideal elevator solution. But Bev, who didn't really like farm life and was known to be scared of chooks, was happy to spend most of her time in the factory with toddler Shelley.

In the early days before they employed staff, Bev did all the packing. The cheeses were packed in the coolroom meaning Shelley got off to a rather cool start in life, calling what came out of the box "cooking monsters." The time it took for the cheese to be manufactured, settled, and packed for delivery was around 10 days. It would then be transported to the marketplace fairly quickly. The shelf life in those days was only 3-4 weeks depending on how consumers looked after and consumed it. As a Frenchman once told George and Bev, "in

France we wait until that white mould has died off and the cheese looks rotten. That's when it's best, but you Australians don't eat it like that. That's the difference between a cheese that has matured and one that hasn't. Cheese keeps on maturing and just gets stronger." Perhaps calling mum or the wife 'the old cheese' isn't such a bad metaphor after all!

Just a normal day making cheese

After the milk was pumped from the dairy and the right butterfat content achieved (standardised), it was pasteurised and placed into 400 litre vats where the cheese maker added the rennet[6] and cultures depending on what cheese he was making. After some time, the milk was turned to a junket, which we call the curd.

The cheese was cut to size in the vats with a wire knife; first one way and then the other to create little square blocks. This allowed the curd and whey to separate leaving a product that looked a lot like junket. A boat winch was used as the handle on the vat and the effluent, that is the whey, was run off from the vat and pumped out onto the pastures. The hoops used to scoop out the curd from the vat were ordinary cooking pots with small holes cut in them and the moulds the curd was 'hooped into' were 100ml PVC pipe cut to size which sat on a removable base. The time to hoop the cheese was critical as if left too long, the curd would solidify in the vats rather than in the moulds. From the moulds, the cheese was placed into a brine bath, later drained and transferred to the maturing room. Here it sat on stainless steel racks designed especially for the task. The cheese making process was always a real team effort.

---

[6] Curdled milk from the stomach of an unweaned calf, containing rennin and used in curdling milk for cheese; a preparation containing rennin.

During the day, the cheese had to be turned about an hour after manufacture and turned again when the pH reached the right level. This was repeated about 3 times during the day and once at night requiring Bev to return to the factory after the kids had gone to bed. When Andrew was old enough, he took this task on. Bev always tried to be home when the kids came home from school balancing and integrating the mountains of work generated from Jindi with family life. Apart from taking charge of the books, Bev also had all the factory washing up to do describing this simply as "a big job." If it's a big job for a Ronalds, you know it really is a big job and the kids were enlisted to help. Every hoop would have cheese stuck in the little draining holes and had to be scrubbed thoroughly in soapy water with a brush, then dipped in the sterilising agent 'Hypo' to get off all the soap, and finally set aside in a sterile environment to dry naturally. Saturday mornings were a big day at Jindi preparing for Monday deliveries but with their faith always prioritised, George and Bev never brought the workers in on Sunday. Andrew regularly worked Saturday mornings and was often assigned the task of washing up the hoops with Bev checking if all the cheese stuck in the draining holes was actually removed. This was a difficult task until George built the washing machine. Who better than George himself to tell the story of the washing machine birthed in the spa.

> One of the biggest headaches that Bev had in the factory was the racks we put the cheese on which looked like the stainless-steel racks you put in the oven. Each one of those racks had two big cheeses on it which were about 12-13 inches across and an inch and half high. As the mould grew, it also grew around the racks so that when you took them off you had all this white mould sticking onto your racks. And it was a rotten job cleaning them. The racks were a real problem to wash and it used to take us all ages. And we didn't really have a fix for it. While Bev and I were up in Queensland with the family one winter I had a

lightbulb moment while we were in a spa. I looked at my hands and thought 'gee, my hands have never been so clean in my life.' I couldn't believe it and a thought struck me: 'I wonder if that will work with the racks'.

So, we came home and we made a machine. We modified a milk vat to take the hot water and detergent and pumped air into it and it boiled the water just like a spa. We made our own crane to lower the racks into it and that crane caused us a bit of trouble later on. I was using it for quite a few years when all the regulations came in and one of the inspectors walked in one day and she said to me 'where's the stamp on that crane that says it can lift the weight?' I said 'what do you mean?' She said 'well who made the crane?' and I said 'I did.' She said 'how do you know it can lift the weight?' and I said 'well it has been for the last 5 years!'

'Oh no' she said, 'you'll have to get that tested by an engineer and make sure it's strong enough'. So, I had to get an engineer in and he laughed and gave me a bit of paper and said it would lift about twice as much weight as we were doing.

As industry became increasingly regulated, this wasn't the first or last time George would face compliance issues with individuals who had less practical experience than himself. At one stage, he had to go to Yallourn TAFE to obtain a Class S Electrical License, which was a Disconnect/Reconnect License. With all the other applicants referred to as 'young fellas' the instructor said to George, "what's a guy your age doing getting his Class S license?" To which George replied, "to legalize what I've been doing all my life!"

George got talking to the instructor and a question was raised about single phase 480-volt power. The instructor maintained there was no such thing. After checking he had heard correctly, George said "well we've got it on our farm" and another bloke undertaking the training said "yeah, we've got it too!" While the city folk in Melbourne only had three-phase (415-volt) or single phase power (240-volt), in the early days three-phase power never went through to rural Victorians. The farmers in attendance were amazed the electrical instructor was totally unaware that most farms were hooked up with 480-volt power produced by connection to 2 x 240-volt circuits.

Having a crack at the big cheese

In 1989 George and Bev purchased an additional 66 acres at Jindivick and it was 1991 when all their hard work, innovation and persevering faith was rewarded and Jindi's first real profit was realised. This was in large part because George never ceased looking for the next opportunity. By chance, or perhaps George might say in response to prayer, he spotted that opportunity in an ad in *The Weekly Times* for the Royal Melbourne Show Cheese Awards. He said to their cheesemaker Craig, "why don't we enter?"

No one really had high expectations. Craig just randomly picked a wheel off the racks to send down to Melbourne and laughed at the suggestion Jindi Cheese might be considered for an award. A few weeks later George and Craig received an invitation to attend the Royal Melbourne Show Dinner and they really had no clue as to why they were personally invited. As George recounts, "we'd never seen silverware like it in our life! They put us near the front and we thought to ourselves what are we doing here! We couldn't believe it."

To their amazement, Jindi Cheese had been awarded Champion Soft Cheese and the Ronalds family were quite overcome by the significance. That sense of wonder can still be seen on George's face and one particular translation of his favourite verse speaks to the moment:

Call to me and I will answer you. I'll tell you marvelous and wondrous

*things that you could never figure out on your own
(Jeremiah 33:3, The Message Bible)*

They certainly hadn't figured awards in!

The Weekly Times quoted one judge declaring their handmade entry was "The best Brie in 20 years at the Show." Given the initial struggles with the farm environment, it was quite ironic that Craig attributed their success in creating the best Brie to the environment it was produced in. As Craig explained to the Herald Sun journalist, "the factory is situated on 100ha farm that supported the cows that supplied the fresh milk. Your larger cheese factories use milk from 500 different farms and they can become a bit plain."

The winning streak would continue and after collecting a swag of awards in 1994, including another Gold Award for its Brie at the Royal Melbourne Show, George told the *Warragul/Drouin Gazette* the company's success could be attributed to a number of things. These included "control over raw materials right from the start of production, and the factory being the only one in Australia designed exclusively for the production of white mould cheese." George's winning business principle is that you "always employ the best person you can, to do the things you can't do."

This initial 1991 win was a great breakthrough for Jindi and gave them a real sales advantage. The business continued to grow in notoriety and to win cheese competitions around the nation at the annual Dairy Classics held in capital cities. George, Bev and sometimes the kids and staff made this annual journey and it was always a memorable and well rewarded event. Jindi stacked up 200 Gold medals, numerous silver medals and other championships at this and many other shows.

Their advertising campaign slogan read 'When you want to strike gold ... ask for Jindi' and it was reported by the *Warragul/Drouin Gazette* after the 1992 Sydney Royal Show that "Jindi Cheese has done exactly what its advertising campaign promotes, it struck gold." In this interview, having confessed to the journalist their first batch of cheese was so bad it had to be dumped in the paddock, George went on to attribute their success to sheer hard work.

There were many people who shared the Jindi journey. Bill Studd, the Butterfields wholesaler and Jindi's distributor was instrumental in opening up the Melbourne markets for them. These were the days before supermarkets had their own deli and people were unfamiliar with soft mould cheeses. Accompanied by toddler Shelley, George and Bev spent a lot of their time demonstrating the Jindi product in Melbourne delis. From the time she could see over the top of the table, Shelley was there handing out cheese samples to curious audiences who would ask questions like "what's the white stuff?" "Is it mould?" "Can we eat it?" Curiosity got the better of many customers who found toddler Shelley's invitation to taste as irresistible as the cheese itself, resulting in increased sales and many more trips to Melbourne.

Given the upturn in business, George was advised by his accountant to take advantage of the season, borrow more money and buy a new car. Things really started moving. Due to the extending sales scope, in 1991 George, his faithful friend Wally and chief engineer Brian O'Connell saw the need to begin the first building extension to the factory. This would be the first of thirteen additional extensions over a twenty-year period of growth that would give the trio years together doing what they were best at; building things. As Wally would say "it was in me to build things strong and good." This would apply to

Wally's friendship with George just as much as his famous fences and factory extensions.

Free enough to make life fun

Whether it was work, family, friendship or his faith journey, George made it fun. Perhaps this is why the advice offered by motivational speaker Brad Cooper at a CEO's seminar in Melbourne resonated so much with him. George recalls with great clarity Brad getting the attention of participants to share some "very valuable advice"… "Never ever let the little boy die inside you … feed it for all its worth, cultivate it, look after it." George always did his best there. Despite all the demands of launching a new business, George always fed the boy within making life fun and exciting. He later confessed his biggest challenges were the increasing rules and regulations he was confronted with. This wasn't the world he was raised in.

With his boyhood love for dozers never diminishing, uncontainable sense of adventure and not being intellectually inhibited by notions that something 'can't be done', entrepreneurial George continued to leave his mark on the local landscape.

The council approval for Jack Cuthbertson's company to provide the earthworks needed to flatten a hill known as 'Ronalds Hill' was reported in the *Warragul Gazette* 30 March 1993. This offered George another opportunity to get back on his beloved bulldozers and scrapers to work with Mick, who he'd started working with 25 years previous. This was all part of a rebuild of the Old Telegraph Road to make it more suitable for fully laden quarry trucks and milk tankers. George recalls the day he and Mick went into Jack's office.

> So we went and sat in Jack's office which consisted of one table,

note book and one pencil and we sat with the shire engineer. Jack said to him 'Well I'll tell you what we'll do. We'll put a 12-foot cut through the top for $12,000 or a 14-foot cut through for $14,000'. The shire engineer said that sounded good to him and asked when we could start. This was two weeks before Easter and we said we'll start on Monday. He said we couldn't start then because we only had 10 days before Easter to work. But we told him we'd have it finished by then. He just looked and smiled and said 'why not?' So, he agreed that they would come and grade for us, take all the levels, and we would do the work. We worked for the first week and didn't see any sign of them at all. The Tuesday before Easter came along and we rang the shire and said 'you better come out and have a look at this road'. And they said 'oh, we forgot all about it'. So, Jack and another Shire Engineer came out and had a look at it. They asked us where all the pegs were so they could take some levels. I said 'what pegs?' They'd all gone! So, the engineer just looked and asked Jack what he thought. We all agreed it looked pretty good and that it would do. Jack told us to just tidy it up and they'd put some metal on it and call it quits'. So, we did and it was open before Easter. That was the sort of thing you could do in those days. We just done it!"

The only survey equipment George used on this job was the naked eye. And it hadn't often failed them.

Andrew gets the experience of a lifetime

By 1994 Jindi had grown to 11 employees. Before Andrew had left university to join the family business full time, George had organized for him to go to Albury for further practical business experience. But to his father's delight and credit, Andrew asked to stay on staff at home. He told his dad, "where else could I get such good experience than working with you?" Of course, it was a truism apparent to all, except perhaps George.

Jindi didn't just offer cheesemaking experience. In this DIY environment insights into construction, plumbing and electrical practicalities were on offer with George providing a whole lot of life, business, networking, sales and team building skills to boot. Having been won over by his son's reasoning that he should gain the necessary management experience *within* the Jindi team, George made just one condition. He insisted that Andrew be on the floor cheesemaking with the boys for the first 6 months which he thoroughly enjoyed. Jindi prided itself in the handmade cheesemaking tradition and as a hands-on type of guy, Andrew didn't see this as a problem. But he couldn't foresee what a problem this would actually be for those hands of his.

For some reason, contact with the whey in the cheesemaking process reacted very badly with Andrew's skin and his hands became super itchy, peeled and were in a real mess. This meant he had to wear gloves the whole time, which for a cheesemaker was not the norm and made the process more difficult. Hands were normally sterilized rather than gloved because knowing the right time to hoop the cheese into the moulds was done by feel. Nevertheless, Andrew persevered as a cheesemaker by day and business development manager by night and computerised the books previously managed manually by Bev. Andrew's superior communication skills proved to be a great asset dealing with the younger sales people and by about 2000, he stepped into the CEO role. This freed up George as Chairman to spend a bit more time outdoors in hands on roles where he preferred to be; building extensions and enjoying his beloved machinery. For all the successful leadership and innovation George provided the Jindi team, George himself was never a cheesemaker. He instinctively met the challenges of the new business by employing the best people he could to undertake the things he recognised he wasn't qualified to do. Having laid the foundation and built both a successful team and cheesemaking business, he would see Jindi wondrously catapult onto the world stage as one of the finest among them. Yet George was always happiest outdoors with his dozers. While Bev referred to her husband as a businessman, George always thought of himself as a farmer and earthmover.

From Jindivick to Wisconsin

It was in 1996 when the Australian Dairy Corporation invited Jindi to put a cheese in the Biennial World Championships held in Wisconsin. George's vision was to produce a quality Australian cheese to compete with all the imports so this seemed a good chance to test Jindi's cheeses against world standards and give the French connoisseurs a run for their milk.

It was decided to enter the Jindi Big Brie in the World Championships and it was *De Ja Vu* Royal Melbourne Show as the Jindi team promptly forgot all about their entry. Then one day, on a regular trip to Melbourne in the Jindi Cheese van, this ordinary day was quickly transformed into an unforgettable one. George received 'the call' from Andrew.

"Dad, pull over ... we just won Champion Soft Mould Cheese of the World!"

It was unthinkable. The local bloke, farmer and earthmover from Jindivick, had just overcome the French masters on the world stage and become a big mover and connoisseur of the world's finest cheese. Jindi Cheese was an overnight international Gold Medal champion. It wasn't just a first for Jindi but the first-time Australian cheeses had ever been successful in the competition.

As George sat on the side of the road that day trying to take it all in, those words from Jeremiah must have been ringing in his ears: *I'll tell you marvelous and wondrous things that you could never figure out on your own.*

The Jindi staff were all jubilant and employee Barry Charlton, who would later start his own cheese factory, was reported in The Star as 'revelling in the success'. Barry confirmed there wasn't any window dressing on their entry, it was virtually a sample pulled off the shelf. Like every other handcrafted Jindi sample, it clearly had two defining characteristics; the human touch and taste of the divine.

When George returned home from Melbourne after receiving Andrew's fateful call, his teenage daughters Narelle and Shelley were keen to know if this meant a trip to Disneyland for them. They weren't disappointed. Narelle was in year 12 and Shelley in Year 8 when George, Bev and the girls made that first trip to America and the acceptance and kindness shown by the Americans toward them left a lasting impression on the whole family.

The 12 international judges who assessed more than 780 entries from 18 countries made comments about how tiny the Jindi factory was. They were amazed the milk being used was almost exclusively from George's 200 cows on the property or cousin Lloyd's pure bred Jersey herd nearby which produced the Triple Cream cheese. This just wasn't done in the United States. George maintained the taste, purity and pure eating pleasure of Jindi's Bries and Triple Creams were the result of their old-fashioned, hand-made cheese manufacturing processes. You can't argue with a Gold Medal!

This initial victory on the world stage was only the beginning. In 2002 Jindi not only won the World Champion Soft Mould Cheese, but after all the champion cheese winners from the different categories were lined up, Jindi took out the award of World Champion Cheese. This was the year they became the champion of champions!

> Moments like this don't happen for everyone! Friends came over with us and we were in a huge auditorium in Wisconsin with 600 cheesemakers from around the world. Bev and I were about ¾ of the way back in the room. When Jindi Cheese was announced, everyone stood to their feet and clapped us all the way to the front. It was overwhelming. I still get emotional about it. That gave me an opportunity to respond and the last thing I said was '… and lastly I want to thank my heavenly Father who enabled me to do this.' So many people came up afterwards and told me how they appreciated what I'd said there.

George never forgot where his help came from.

While quick to acknowledge Jindi's champion cheesemakers who contributed to the 2002 award, George and Bev declined to nominate an individual cheesemaker. This wasn't due to any lack of appreciation. As Bev said "we reckoned it's not the cheesemaker, it's the team. The farmers had supplied the milk, the cheesemaker had turned the curd by day but somebody else had turned it at night. Somebody else added ingredients and somebody else packed the cheese." There were a lot of somebody else champions in the process. They maintained "there is no individual cheese maker." So Jindi Cheese did something unique. They took the award as a team, not as an individual cheesemaker, breaking the mould of award protocol.

There was another great win in 2004 when Jindi was again awarded Champion White Mould Cheese. George, Bev, Andrew and their cheesemaker all made their way to Wisconsin to receive this third World Championship. Despite all the international accolades, the farmer from Jindivick maintained their biggest moment was actually that very first award at the Melbourne Showgrounds in 1991 that had given them the initial breakthrough.

By 2003 Jindi Engineering, an adjunct to Jindi Cheese employing the expertise of Brian O'Connell, was also humming along. Brian and George's brother Alan had previously supervised the manufacture of the steel work for a large Youth Hall at Warragul Community Church. With this under their belt in 2000, the aside engineering business was positioned for the bigger projects taking responsibility for the steelwork in the remodelling of the Belgrave Heights Convention Centre auditorium. With a seating capacity of 2,000 this extension incorporated about 40 tonnes of heavy steelwork used in the manufacture of complicated angles and beams. Like George, the central commitment of the Belgrave Heights Convention Centre was to serve the church making support of this project much more than just an aside venture. Whether brick by brick, post by post, or frame by frame, George was always a man to pull up his sleeves and put his muscle where his heart was.

"We don't sell to supermarkets"

That first World Championship in 1996 opened up new markets. Jindi was selling to Menora Foods and created another brand called Wattle Valley that opened up an even bigger market than Jindi. Coles, and later Woolworths, both approached Jindi. But George as a self-confessed big country boy said to Coles "we don't sell to supermarkets, we sell to delis." Even when they came back a second-time George remained faithfully resolute simply responding "didn't you hear me the first time."

It was Butterfields, who had assisted Jindi's marketing to Melbourne from the beginning, that gave George a bit of sound advice. Jindi was still selling to Butterfields in 1996 when one of their representatives returned from America. He told George the Americans were putting big cheese cabinets in the supermarkets and he predicted this would happen in Australia too. George was advised to make portions rather than just the big wheels they were selling to delis at the time.

With this new advice, when Woolworths came back to George the next time he told them "we better talk about this!" George knew who to listen to and this served him well throughout his business career. Woolworths offered George free shelf space but in return he was asked to make a 'Stabilized Product' i.e. Jindi would have to cut the wheel, wedge it and dry wrap it. This introduced them to plastic packaging which vacuum sealed the wedges.

After Woolworths, Coles also came back to Jindi opening a different market to them again. But Jindi continued selling to delis in the traditional way describing it as *the cream*. "Once you go into supermarkets it's a very different market and not as good a product. On a big wheel cheese matures differently than it does if you cut it and wedge it." So Jindi would wrap the product for the convenience of people purchasing a wedge at the supermarket but maintained that the cheese not wrapped in plastic and sold in larger portions at the deli was better quality. George maintains if you want really good quality cheese you "go to the deli and they cut if off the wheel for you there…Things may have changed today but at that time the taste was considerably different." Connoisseurs take note!

This new avenue of business resulted in substantial growth for Jindi and they were now able to buy their own truck. They had advanced from a van that wasn't even refrigerated to an air-conditioned refrigerated 3-tonne truck and were well on their way toward that next step when they'd be using semi-trailers.

George referred to the supermarket as a tough market, but when it came to business negotiations, George was no woose himself.

Before they had the Jindi brand on their shelves, the supermarkets were stocking the Jindi produced Wattle Valley brand which they sourced from Menora Foods. George was aware the supermarkets were desperate to add Jindi Cheese as a new line and he used this to his advantage. Wattle Valley was always a cheaper product and a little lower class. George wanted a price rise on it and so told Coles he wanted a rise of $1 per kilo on Wattle Valley. George was told by the salesman it was already too dear but rather than be intimidated, he flexed up. "If I don't get it, I'll withdraw my product from you." The salesman told George he couldn't do that but George knew better. "It's my product; I can do what I want to." He used the Jindi product as leverage and it paid off. While the salesman wanted a caveat on the deal stipulating if sales started to drop off there'd be a return to the old price what actually happened is George got his $1 rise and the salesman got the sack! The big guys, the big vision, the big machinery – none of it was intimidating to this Jindivick farmer.

With both Wattle Valley and Jindi brands now in the supermarket (essentially the same product in different wrapping) Menora Foods came to George and said "Brie sells better in Sydney than what Camembert does…do you think you can make a small Brie for us." George replied "no problem…we'll change the labels!" That's what they did and this opened up another new market. Having said that, George acknowledges that different cultures can be used to distinguish between the cheeses.

This simple solution was actually informed advice and George shared a little bit of history to explain why. A French cheese maker had once come into the Jindi factory and George asked him to explain the difference between Brie and Camembert. He discovered the only real difference came from a strong difference of opinion between two brothers. Brie was from a town in France called by that name and was first made in big wheels by two brothers around 1217. One day they had an argument and so the younger brother left and set up 60 km south in a town called Camembert. He questioned why they should only make big wheels and decided to take the recipe and make small wheels. He called his small wheels Camembert. The result was Brie was made in big wheels in Brie and Camembert in small wheels in Camembert. While a big wheel will mature differently to a small wheel, the Frenchman told George "you people in Australia have mucked the whole industry up because you have made a 1kg Brie and a little Brie but there's no such thing; its either a Brie or a Camembert!"

Those distinctions are maintained in competitions. Jindi made front page news in the Warragul Gazette for taking out the National Cheese Competitions in both Brie and Camembert categories, but as George confessed, they used the same culture for both. It was a winning recipe.

The Jindi business recipe was just as successful as its cheese recipe. They employed a lot of locals and Craig as the head cheesemaker was ultimately supported by 4-5 other cheesemakers. The packing room alone would often have 10-15 people busy at work. The kids from the church who were in Year 11 or 12 were also involved and a lot of the university students worked in their holidays which helped them get through those student years. The Ronalds kids were all heavily involved and to their credit, earnt enough from it to help put themselves through university.

One of the most labour intensive, part-time afterhours tasks, was folding the cheese boxes. The Chief Box Folder was Glen Treble who was often ribbed by co-workers for what he and Jenny

Ronalds might be up to behind those boxes; romance was brewing. Glen took over Jenny's box folding duties when she headed off to university in Sydney to study music for 12 months. After returning, she took on the part-time role of supervisor in the packing room with Bev. While at university himself, Glen continued as part-time box-folder gaining the reputation as a human machine. On the 12 December 2001, Glen recorded a massive output folding 3,250 Camembert boxes in a single 8-hour day. This was the most boxes ever folded in a day at Jindi and it wasn't just to impress Jenny, who he successfully wooed and married. Glen still reminds his father-in-law that he paid them all 10cents a box and so working hard and fast was driven by this monetary incentive. None of the local kids employed would be calling for a go slow! Bev knew in advance how many boxes she needed to pack for end-of-week deliveries giving Glen a lot of flexibility about the hours he kept over his impressive 10-year box folding career. Being involved with Tender Care, who supported people with disabilities, Glen would often opt to fold boxes on weekends or evenings for the extra cash. With a gleeful smile and chuckle, George recalled the last day Glen folded boxes for them in the box room. "Glen actually filled the whole room 'chock a block' and when the girls opened the door the next morning a heap of boxes tumbled out."

Jindi was not only a family business with invested family memories, Jindi also invested in building community memories. This gold standard for life and business saw Jindi Cheese awarded the 2001 Gippsland Business of the Year, both the main award and the Export Category. This was testimony to the economic investment made to the Gippsland region with many people acknowledging, the social and cultural capital they invested would be infinitely greater.

Topping it off with Blue

As the Jindi expertise grew so did their product range. In the early days Jindi didn't produce Blue Cheese but being experts at spotting opportunity, they recognised the growing demand to add this to their range. Not far away in a little town called Bena was another pioneer of the early speciality cheese making industry: Top Paddock Cheeses. Fred Leppin was the founder and owner and by 1999 he was ready to retire. Negotiations began and after much discussion Jindi purchased Top Paddock the same year. Their great range of cheese was continued and Jindi began further development of blue cheeses. Jindi Blue took a number of years to develop but eventually won many awards and was available across Australia through delicatessens, Coles and Woolworths. In the mid 2000s the old factory at Bena was eventually closed and all production moved to the main Jindivick site where it is still made today.

Dipping into yet another market

About the same time, Jindi moved into dip manufacturing. Andrew worked on this project with the General Manager of Menora, John Algeri. Once again there was a lot of development work and a dedicated team effort with particular help from Alec Zurrer who was added to the Jindi team. It was expected that dips would really take off just as the European cheeses had and Jindi was up for the challenge.

While the expertise for cheesemaking was found in France, the best machines used to make dips were made in England. A lot of research had gone into finding the right machine and by an amazing coincidence, it turned out that the best was made by Coates Engineering in England, very distant relatives of Bev. There were already 2-3 operators in Australia making dips but as George knew, they could hardly go to these Australian factories and ask to see how they operated them.

Andrew contacted the English manufacturer discovering the only factory that would let them in to see their machine operation and share the needed intel was just below Nazareth in Israel. George was extremely enthusiastic about going so with Andrew and Alec Zurrer, they took off to Israel. It was a memorable flight and being before 9/11, they were all able to get a birds-eye view from the cockpit as they flew over Iraq.

The trio found the Israelis were very good about sharing information. After being shown through their factory and obtaining the needed recipes, they all decided to spend a few extra days with them and allow the pages of the Bible to come alive. Their friendly escort was named Mickey and he shared interesting insights as they went to Caesarea, the Garden of Gethsemane and Hezekiah's Tunnel. Hezekiah's Tunnel is described in the Bible in II Chronicles 32 and was discovered in 1867 by explorer Sir Charles Warren. The tunnel, with a creek flowing through it, was wide enough to walk through leading to the Pool of Siloam in the original site of Jerusalem. That's the pool where Jesus had sent the blind man to wash the mud out of his eyes and have his sight restored. George was certainly fascinated with the excavation job, a narrow tunnel 350 metres long begging the question how they got the material out. But he was also fascinated by the depth of history in the region and the thought that he was treading along the same roads the greatest earthmover of all had walked. George being George, he was also fascinated to see the Uzi submachine guns the Arab guards donned.

After ordering the dip machine from England, Brian, George and Wally began to build a special factory for it. This meant another extension which took a couple of years to complete. By 2005, the dips were just starting to really take off. Andrew and George anticipated they would be bigger in volume than cheese sales. But the wind of change was blowing.

The end of an era

It was August 2004 when Danny Gluck, son of the founder of Menora Foods, approached George and Andrew. Danny told them they ought to cement their relationship. Up to this point there was only a handshake agreement between them. Danny wanted to buy 20% of Jindi. At the time, Menora constituted about 60% of the Jindi business and Jindi contributed greatly to theirs. Danny's son was coming into the business at this stage and asking about Menora's relationship with Jindi. It was clear it needed to be formalised. George found himself uttering that throwaway line he had put out there years earlier: "no way, it's all or nothing!" The 'all or nothing' guy was himself surprised when Danny shot back asking "how much is all?"

Jindi had been approached by other companies before including some of Australia's largest producers. Andrew and George talked about it. Since Andrew had taken on the CEO role, George was left to concentrate on being Chairman. Unsurprisingly, the main chair George enjoyed was the one on his dozer. Andrew pointed out to his dad that at 68 he couldn't expect him to keep going on outside doing all the work he was doing forever; climbing ladders, building extensions, and doing all the maintenance and steel work. And the rules and regulations around business and buildings were getting very tight. It wasn't the same era George was raised in. Back in the day if you wanted to push a tree over, you just pushed it over.

Andrew said "I rely on you as much as you rely on me dad. You have to realize, if you're in business, selling is part of it."

Jindi now had the extension plans to double the size of the plant from 1500 square metres up to 3,000. This would require several million dollars and they had just started the earthworks. The farmland was an important consideration in the proposed sale of Jindi. It was important to keep the factory effluent (i.e. the whey) in reserve May – October in order not to saturate the land in the wet winter months and have it ready to pump over the farm in the dry summer months.

Rules and regulations had always challenged George and it would be the rules and regulations governing the final decision by the Environmental Protection Authority (EPA), that would constitute George's ultimate challenge. The EPA concluded that the land used for effluent purposes couldn't be separated from the farm. The business, the factory and the much-loved farmland must be sold as a unit. It really was an all or nothing deal.

George and Bev once again chose 'all'. In 2005 with 80+ staff, Jindi Cheese was sold to wholesaler Menora Foods. The total transaction took nearly twelve months being sealed with a hand shake between Andrew and Menora's John Algeri. It was a deeply emotional time for George and the Ronalds family, yet they recognized it was time to enter a new season. The good book says there is indeed a time for everything, and a season for every activity under heaven. Timing was everything. George had seen others hang onto their business's for too long and in his mind the idea of selling a business was to sell on the crest of a wave, from where a bigger view is possible.

After the sale, George and Andrew had a final opportunity to ride that wave for a little longer as Menora contracted them to finish the earthworks they'd begun. With George on Peter Cuthbertson's big Fiat-Ellis HD30 340 H.P dozer and Andrew on the HD11 bulldozer, they began construction of a huge 20-acre-foot dam for effluent purposes. An acre-foot dam is not a measurement we are all familiar with. This represents enough water to cover an acre of land, about the size of a football field, one foot deep making a 20-acre-foot-dam a substantial farm project. The effluent was pumped out onto the pasture during the summer months.

To level the ground for the new extension, George transported 3,000 truck and trailer loads of fill (that's 80,000 tonnes) from Peter Cuthbertson's quarry across the road. That's a lot of dirt! Despite this sure foundation, an engineer acting on behalf of Menora, threw into question whether the fill was solid. George was rightly concerned they might be required to pull it all out so he had it tested. This confirmed the fill was harder than the ground beneath it and that the experience of the farmer, who'd been making fill all his life, had outperformed the engineer!

The farmer plants the seed ...

George as a farmer understood well the profound Biblical truths expressed in agricultural terms for first century audiences. At the end of an era in his life, the sentiments expressed in John 12:24 had particular relevance.

> *Unless a kernel of wheat falls to the ground and dies, it remains only a single seed. But if it dies, it produces many seeds.*

George had planted many seeds on this land. Like his father before him, he had been raised on it, cleared it, farmed it, built his home on it, raised his own family on it and poured his life into it. And he still marvels at what it produced. From this remote family business tucked away near the tiny town of Jindivick, he had found himself flung onto the world stage as a champion producer. George understood it wasn't all about him and that it wasn't all over. Future champions could be produced to bring benefits to the town, industry and nation. But a personal sacrifice, a death of sorts, would be required. Letting go of the land he'd invested his whole life into was just that. George knew he had to let go of it all but he also understood some eternal truths. That in this life, what he'd produced would last forever and the 'all' he was letting go of was 'all temporary anyway.' By selling Jindi, George and Bev were able to do things they couldn't do before and help the family like never before. A well-deserved new season was upon them.

With Menora Foods on-selling to Lactalis about 3 years later, the Jindi legacy of growth and excellence continued to produce gold. George confessed that Menora as a wholesaler could never really get their heart and head around manufacturing. The manufacturing and wholesaling approaches to cheesemaking proved to be distinctly different.

Jindi Cheese is still owned by Lactalis today, the biggest private dairy company in the world with a $15B Euro turnover. In 2015 Lactalis had 75,000 employees globally and is a diary company based in the heart of western France's dairy region. It seems fitting that Jindi, inspired by the French masters of fine cheeses, should end its journey embraced by those masters. With the Jindi seed planted where it can increase exponentially, this was definitely not the end of a legacy.

The French Lactalis predicted a lot more investment in Jindi affirming the plan was to develop the business, not to shut it down. In letting go of the business and farmland, George did let go a piece of himself much like a seed that dies. But in so doing, Jindi certainly did produce many more seeds resulting in more community goodwill, more jobs and growth in the local economy. And the Gold Medal Award Standard set by the Ronalds family and Jindi team live on.

Jindi advertising

4

Black Saturday: George, the Bushfires and the Battlers

According to the CFA website: "The 2009 bushfires in January and February ravaged many parts of Victoria and touched directly and indirectly many millions of people in the State, across Australia and internationally. One hundred and seventy-three people died, thousands of homes and other dwellings were destroyed and over 400,000 hectares were burnt".

According to Dr Kevin Tolhurst, senior lecturer fire ecology at Melbourne University, this was a firestorm so powerful that the heat "equalled about 500 atomic bombs landing on Hiroshima..."[7]

The temperatures were over 1400^C (2552^F) with winds in excess of 120kph (70 mph) stirring up 100 metre (300 ft) high flames consuming everything and everybody in their path.

Over 5,000 brave firefighters fought united against this gargantuan firestorm assault. Having worked the land, built his home on it, and

---

[7] Karen Kissane, "Black Saturday fires equal to 1500 atomic bombs: expert", *The Sydney Morning Herald*, 22 May 2009.

poured his life into it, at 72 years old, George Oscar Ronalds joined those brave firefighters to defend it.

Black Saturday in Jindivick

7 February, 2009 was a Saturday cauterized in George's mind. In the early afternoon, thick darkness and smoke fell upon his property as the firestorm raged all around. The power was out and he was trapped in the family home with his brother Dave and three friends; Andrew Pike, Justin (Juzz) Wallace and Mark Dunsmiur. The only light they could see from the house was unsightly; leaping flames threatening to engulf them all. George's brother Dave addressed him soberly. 'We've been through a lot together George and it looks like we're going to die together.' In their current predicament, this seemed a likely outcome. Juzz rang his girlfriend to say 'good bye.'

A lightning strike in the Bunyip State Forest about 25km to the west had ignited this fire the previous Monday but it was thought the DSE (Department of Sustainability & Environment) had it under control and had extinguished it on Tuesday. But by Thursday, as smoke started to rise again, it was clear this wasn't the case. By Friday the smoke became increasingly ominous. You don't need to tell Victorians the obvious; where there's smoke there's fire.

To make matters worse, this was a fire with plenty of fuel. January had been the lowest rainfall on record with only 4mls recorded following a wet spring with exceptional growth. The last week in January the temperatures had been up to 45 degrees with low humidity. This was followed by a very dry start to February; a week without rain at all. The country side was tinder dry and looked ready to explode. Resident Gippslanders knew they could be in for a lot of trouble.

This was confirmed on Friday at the local CFA meeting where George and others were warned of the extreme danger. The forecast for the next day was indeed threatening; 45-degree heat, low humidity with strong gale force winds. Everyone understood this was a recipe for disaster and George and Bev's property was in the line of fire.

Nevertheless, on that fateful Saturday morning George kept up his regular routine and early morning meeting with church elders. That is, until 8am, by which time he knew he'd have to rush home. Once there George could see the fire was starting to move and it was time to make fire breaks around the sheds, house and fence lines. George called Peter Cuthbertson to borrow his power grader and got to work.

By early afternoon the extensive fire breaks around his and Dave's farm were done. With angry black smoke billowing overhead, George knew they better get back to the house and factory, and park the grader in a safe place. First the cattle were rounded up into the yards with water sprinklers above them.

One act of kindness followed another and a sprinkling of assistance from above in the form of Andrew, Juzz and Mark came for George as well. The three friends from Warragul came to help out and were critical characters in what would become George's own 'Famous Five' adventure story. With the extra hands the labor could be divided to cover home and factory. It was decided George's son Andrew and factory manager Andrew Bohni, would stay down at the Jindi factory. The three Warragul helpers would remain with George and take the fire truck up to the house. From here they had a good view of the surrounding country side and it was a frightening sight.

To the West the swelling inferno was unfolding filling the sky with voluminous black smoke. Being fully fueled as it came out of the forest, the fiery beast was able to outrun the CFA as they fled from its path. The fire captain later relayed to George how he feared for those ahead as it passed him fleeing the forest.

As the trapped men wet-down everything surrounding the house, they kept their eyes fixed on the firestorm. Great sheets of consuming red flame leapt forward, sometimes jumping hundreds of meters at a time. The men knew to look up and were rewarded with a welcome sight. Elvis the fire helicopter was spotted in the distance, dropping huge volumes of water on houses and sheds giving some hope. It wasn't just the cattle that needed a sprinkling.

Dave's farm was next to George's and Dave had been yarding up bullocks there on the east side. However, he couldn't go out that way as the fire was already burning past his place. Leaving his son Jason and son-in-law Dan to round up the bullocks on 'Sleeps Hill' – the farm to the west – Dave joined George and the Warragul trio. Meanwhile the fire continued to approach at an alarming speed.

Dave's exit was timely. As they watched from 600 meters away, his hay shed and silage bales exploded in a ball of flame. Then the fire roared like a jet plane as it sped up the hill towards them. The five could see the flames twice the height of the trees leaping in front of them. It was so intense to be enveloped in the heat both above and around. George noted that it had taken less than a minute for the fire to cover the distance from Dave's shed. He immediately shouted to the others "GET INSIDE."

Bev had already left the home about an hour earlier having done her best to ready things for the battlers left behind. All the windows and doors were closed and she left towels soaking in the tub. These would be run along the bottom of doors as resistance to sparks seeking an entry point. It was indeed a black day and with the power out, the men had to use torches to find their way around the house.

George rang 000 to alert emergency workers they were trapped in the house and advised them Elvis was nearby; although he later discovered Elvis had been diverted to an outbreak in Warragul. Juzz rang his girlfriend to say good bye and Dave uttered those sobering words: "We've done a lot together George and it looks like we're going to die together." The garden was being consumed by the firestorm and so was all hope. Just for a moment, time seemed to stand still.

However, time doesn't stand still and nothing was standing still outside. Jolted by an enormous noise, the five peered out the window. The LPG gas cylinder was venting behind the garage. It was shooting a frightening 50-foot flame into the air. When the smoke cleared for a few seconds, this created an eerie break in the smoke like a bright light from above. This pot of light enabled George to see the fire truck. Sitting on burnt out ground, he could hardly believe it was still intact. He ran out and found the pump motor was still running so opened the throttle and began cooling the LPG cylinder.

The excitement of having water to play with was short lived. The heat was unbearable and George was forced back inside. With the fire now raging inside the garage only 5 metres from the house, it seemed inevitable that it would be consumed.

Having been in constant touch with Andrew, George knew that the factory still offered a place of refuge and the men decided to make their way through the smoke to reach it, describing the experience as moving through thick darkness all the way. The conversations between the men also reflected the darkness that hung over them.

Dave shared how he'd left his two sons earlier in the afternoon to yard the bullocks. With the fire having now been through the region and the boys being uncontactable, he wasn't sure they'd survived. It was like something out of a movie when the boys later came walking out of the smoke to join them. Dan had jumped into the dam and Jason decided to drive the tractor through the fire on to the safety of already burnt ground. George attributed their survival to miraculous intervention. They had been 'looked after.'

Sometime between 5 and 6pm when the fury of the fire seemed to have passed, George and Andrew headed back to see what was left of the family home. Although the wind had died down, there was still plenty of smoke and burning embers around.

Approaching the house, they could see the garden was completely ravaged and destroyed by the fire and Shelly's new car was reduced to a shell. Alloy melts at 1500 degrees and Shelly's alloy wheels were melted on the shattered concrete garage floor. The concrete water tank was also shattered. All that remained of George's chainsaw was the bar. As George cast his eyes upon the house he was once again overcome by the sentiments echoed in Jeremiah 33:3 'I called; You answered.' This isn't just a banner over his desk or a platitude for George, it is literally the testimony of his life.

Not only was the house still standing, on closer inspection they couldn't find any damage at all, not even a paint blister! Both the family home and the Jindi Cheese factory had miraculously escaped unharmed.

With the red glow from spot fires all around them, Andrew and George slept in the family home that Saturday night. George thought the glowing surrounds looked like fairy land. It had been a very long and intense day in the heat and smoke, with the men working well into the night with the CFA. Yet, as he reflected on the day, George couldn't recall being thirsty or hungry. He was grateful for many things including the opportunity to see the Jindi factory used as both a refuge and a resource. The big Jindi tanks and fire pumps had been busy filling the CFA fire trucks. The glow without was matched by a grateful glow within. George was grateful to be alive to see another day. He wasn't concerned about the lack of power to his house that night. It was just comforting to be there and so they slept.

Perhaps ignorance is bliss. When the power was restored to his house the following Tuesday, half the house was still without power. George called in an electrician and it was then he realized he and Andrew had probably continued to keep a few angels busy that Saturday night. The electrician found several metres of burnt wire in the ceiling and a lot of charred insulation.

As the smoke cleared on Sunday morning, George was faced with a very depressing sight. There were thousands of acres of blackened paddocks, trees and burnt fences. Four homes on Old Telegraph Road, including their share farm house, and many sheds were also burnt. George, Andrew and the Jindi fire truck got to work and Sunday was spent mopping up fires. By evening they were exhausted and Andrew went home. George went into Warragul to pick up Bev who was at their daughter Jenny's place. After a good meal, hot shower and a couple of hours together, George and Bev headed home.

Driving in tandem, they were forced to stop on the way at a road block. The Police wouldn't allow George to go any further due to another outbreak on Old Telegraph Road. George tried to convince the Police that as he was local and familiar with the landscape and fire drill he should be able to proceed. The policeman, however, wasn't a local one or willing to give George the free pass he was looking for. Necessity being the mother of invention, George privately told Bev to follow him and despite the roadblock, within fifteen minutes they were home again. The fires were still burning in the district and Bev was shocked to see the devastation firsthand.

The following day was Monday and friends arrived in the morning with food supplies for them. David Hobbs also turned up and fixed the brakes on the fire truck enabling Andrew and George to continue putting out fires for another 2 days. Sometimes they worked independently and sometimes with the CFA crew. It was a mammoth cooperative effort and would take 10 days for the fire to be completely extinguished.

Community volunteerism and generosity was notable. There was so much to repair and rebuild yet George wasn't overwhelmed by this but by the people who flocked in to help with the enormous cleanup. Fifteen people arrived on his farm on the Wednesday including some George didn't even know. To meet the fencing challenges, one man arrived with his tractor and post driver. Trailer loads of posts arrived and so did coils of barb wire. Casting regulatory restrictions aside, George jumped on his bulldozer and cleared fence lines of trees. The team spirit was tangible with the men working for several days on the cleanup and fencing. Bev and others worked hard to provide the meals enabling the men to complete the boundary fences and even start on some internal fencing. George and Bev remain grateful to all who helped their swift recovery from the firestorm.

Physical repairs are one thing but emotional and spiritual repair was also needed. One way this was met was through the compassion of Jack Mundy and Danny from the 'Billy Graham Rapid Response Team' who came and visited all the people who were involved and impacted by the fire. Jack Mundy addressed residents in a public meeting at the Warragul Community Church. He told them "There will be a new normal for you. Whenever you see a wisp of smoke, your minds will go back to the fire". As George said; "He was right. Nearly ten years later, this is still true."

Teams from George's church were also actively helping others in the adjacent Labertouche district. They spent many months there providing residents with much-needed support and from this a local community church emerged.

As one of the five trapped in the house on Black Saturday, George is convinced he was looked after from above and inserts his own name in the book he loves next to a number of Biblical verses:

> Psalm 121:28: The Lord will watch over your coming and going both now and forevermore
>
> Deuteronomy: 33:27 The Eternal God is my refuge and underneath are the everlasting arms

These are everlasting and living words for George and longevity in George's story is not restricted to words alone. While the Jindi Fire Truck may not be everlasting, it did outlive the fire and still stands as a testament of perseverance in Pa's Shed at the Ronalds' residence on Main Road, Jindivick. Being fully operational, the fire truck provides wonderful memories for George, a talking point for visitors and entertainment for all; especially George and Bev's grandchildren. Both the story and the Fire Truck live on.

Black Saturday fire approaches

George and mate Wally

Jindi Fire Truck at work

Jindi Farm

Shelley's car

Lloyd and Bruce Ronalds re-fencing

Jindi Cheese factory escaped the fire

5
Beyond 1959: Warragul YFC & Australia's Spiritual Revolution

> The nameless pioneers and settlers, the obscure mothers and fathers, the quiet craftsmen and tradesmen; it is only among these that the real story of America (let's say Australia) is told; it is only among them that the brilliance of liberty may be comprehended.[8]

The quote above reflects the admiration Theodore Roosevelt possessed for 'The Common Man'. One of his favourite contemporary writers, G. K. Chesterton often asserted that 'the most extraordinary thing in the world is an ordinary man and an ordinary woman and their ordinary children.'[9] The course of history is changed by ordinary people and just like the rest of the world, Australia is full of them. The paradox of being both ordinary and extraordinary is part of the great mystery of life. This is a mystery many ordinary people seek to understand. 1959 was such a time.

---

[8] George Grant, *Carry a Big Stick: The Uncommon Heroism of Theodore Roosevelt*, Tennessee, 1996, 122.
[9] Ibid., 123

On the brink of the sexual revolution, there was an extraordinary spiritual revolution for ordinary Australians and in 2009 ABC's 'Compass' presenter Geraldine Doogue aired a special program to commemorate it. The year 2009 was the 50th anniversary of the 4-month nationwide Billy Graham crusade. Doogue reminded her audience that in 1959 well over three million Australians had flocked to hear the American Christian preacher. That represented a staggering 30 per cent of the nation.

Among that 30 percent was 15-year-old Peter Jensen. Jensen was just one of the 57,000 people in Sydney meetings to respond to Graham's invitation to make a commitment to Christ. Jensen would later become the Anglican Archbishop of Sydney. Although at this time nearly 90 percent of Australians already identified as Christian, Jensen pointed out on the Compass program that many would be described as 'nominal'. What he meant was that many were 'cultural Christians' i.e. those who by virtue of being born in a Christian culture identified this way. Jensen said that what Billy Graham did for them was to make Christ personal.

It was a spiritual revolution because it really changed people; some for a few years and some for a lifetime. And it wasn't just those who could get to the city that were impacted. Radio took Billy to the bush with his message being transported into four hundred communities across Australia. Billy Graham's crusade was said to be responsible for a nationwide drop in crime rates, alcohol consumption, and for 3 years afterward a falling number of illegitimate births.[10] That's positive change for the nation and as Roosevelt might say 'the brilliance of liberty'.

Over a period of four weeks 714,000 Victorians went to see Billy

---

[10] ABC Compass, 15 February 2009.

Graham. The final Melbourne meeting was held in the MCG where he preached to the greatest crowd ever to fill the stands. There were 143,000 people crammed into the MCG and speakers were hastily rigged up outside to cater to an additional 4,000 people queued there. There was a spiritual hunger hovering over Melbourne set to rival the 1902 visit from American evangelist, Rev. R. A. Torrey who attracted 117,000 people to his meetings. This too was remarkable given Melbourne's population in 1902 was somewhere between 400-500,000 people.

Farmers, Fencers & Youth Leaders

Billy Graham, the man dubbed 'God's Salesman' by the press, drew ordinary people from all over the state. Two of those ordinary people who travelled in from Gippsland were George Oscar Ronalds and Wally Kenney. While they wouldn't meet for a year or two later, this pivotal event would see their lives providentially linked in a special friendship that would span over 50 years. It wasn't a compartmentalised friendship limited to annual 4WD trips, fishing expeditions or shared family holidays. This was a fully integrated friendship that transcended personal and professional boundaries. George and Wally would work together, play and pray together, and be fisherman of the biblical kind making faith fun for hundreds of young people in regional Victoria. It was because Wally became a Christian in 1959 at that Billy Graham meeting in Melbourne that he was introduced to a whole new circle of people. One of those people was George and together these two rugged outdoor men would model spirituality and manliness to hundreds of young Australians. Most importantly, they would model the Australian ideal of mateship. Quite simply, everything about them was real.

For those who think theologically, it's a little ironic how both these farmers, George the agriculturalist and Wally the horticulturalist, actually met and what they found they had in common. Early in the 1960's before George built the dairy he was clearing land with his brother Dave, and they would spend quite a bit of time splitting posts. He got to know Wally through the fencing business. Wally loved fencing and heard George and Dave were splitting posts so he asked them to split posts for him. It was Wally's super-sized corner posts that really impressed George. Lovers of Theology know that Christ is referred to as the 'chief corner stone' or 'head of the corner'[11] that supporting 'post' that really holds everything together. George and Wally not only found beauty in those extraordinary corner posts in the ground, on a spiritual level, they were destined to share a common love for the 'chief corner stone' as well.

Something else the men shared was a formidable work ethic. They both worked incredibly hard. In the early 1960s Wally Kenney ran a cattle stud and at the same time was a partner with David and Peter Rowse in a very labour intensive business growing flowers. At times, they employed up to 70 staff. Almost every university student in the district would find themselves working for Wally and the Rowse Brothers at some time during their holidays to support those student years. Two of their better-known student labourers were the Costello brothers, Tim and Peter. Tim became the high profile World Vision Advocate and his brother Peter the Federal Treasurer in the Howard Government. Despite their notoriety, their humble beginnings included hand-picking flowers.

After farming all day and often volunteering evenings at the church, Wally would also drive to the Victoria Market in Melbourne

---

[11] The Gospel of Matthew 21:42.

to sell the flowers three nights a week. He would leave Gippsland a little after midnight, deliver to the airport and arrive at the Victoria Market to set up at 3:30am for a 4am opening. Here Wally would remain until his flowers were sold out. With no more than 2 hours sleep, he would then make the long drive home to get back to his farming duties repeating this schedule three times a week. One night Wally was so tired that when he stopped for a red light at a St Kilda Road crossing, he fell into a deep sleep at the lights. Two hours passed while he rested at those lights with his engine running and headlights on, until someone eventually woke him about 2am.

Wally's car engine wasn't the only engine that kept on running. Like thousands of other Australians, he and George were spiritually refueled at that 1959 meeting. While George was raised in a professing Christian home, Wally was the first one in three generations of his family to publicly confess his Christian faith. Yet they responded similarly in their expression of faith with a passion for youth. George was a local Sunday School teacher from the time he was 15 but Wally's was a relatively new faith when he took on the local youth group at Drouin Presbyterian Church. A sense of humour goes a long way with youth and Wally and George would both make faith lots of fun for the kids. They independently took kids to the popular YFC (Youth for Christ) rallies in Melbourne where even adults could be 'big kids'. Billy Graham had been the first full time YFC worker as early as 1943 and he made disciples everywhere he went. The meetings spread like wildfire after the Second World War and while US critics called them a 'hoot n hollering' for Jesus, after his phenomenal Australian Tour, YFC rallies in Melbourne, and around Australia, remained popular through the 60's – to early 90's. YFC meetings started in Melbourne in the Chapter House in St Paul's Cathedral known as 'the dungeon room.' Corrie Ten Boom was just one of the notable speakers inspiring the hungry youth in the dungeon. But YFC couldn't be contained in Melbourne.

It was 1963 when George, Wally, two co-workers and Clive Stebbins, Melbourne YFC Director for 36 years, went to Healesville to meet visiting YFC World President Dr Kelly Bihl. Here these farmers, fencers and youth leaders committed to form Warragul Youth for Christ (WYFC). George and Wally were among its founding members and only 6 months after its inception, George took on the role as the Warragul Director.

Rally Ministry was a big deal in YFC culture until the early 1990s with rallies being the entry point for most youth. While this was before the days of contemporary church bands, music teams were at every rally playing the most up to date Christian music of the time. There were also trained youth councillors and George found the response rate to the message increased as they increased the number of councillors. By way of oversight there were also advisors like George who were appointed to ensure that the youth understood what their decision to follow Christ meant; that they knew what they'd actually done, and to ensure they weren't just swept up in an emotional moment by a persuasive young councillor. It was also the councillor's role to take responsibility for follow up after the rallies. This ministry was known as 'Follow Through Care' and helped all the youth to find a spiritual home. Discipleship was extremely important and attributed for the high retention rate of young people in YFC.

George was never the front man or a speaker at these youth rallies, and was never on the platform. He wasn't a pastor but a farmer and earthmover, trained on a bulldozer. George always directed in the background with Wally right behind him setting up, organising the flowers, preparing the BBQ, and very much hands on for the clean up afterwards. They were an effective team.

After it was formed, the WYFC decided to have a rally on the second Saturday of every second month with the first one scheduled for 14 September 1963. The guest speaker at this inaugural Warragul rally was the young man Brian Willersdorf who was about 21 at the time. Rev Dr Brian Willersdorf would consequently be referred to as 'Australia's Billy Graham' for attracting many thousands of Australians. One of the many thousands that happened to hear his preaching in that first Warragul rally at St Andrews Presbyterian Hall later became the Bishop of Hobart. WYFC had a permanent booking at the Presbyterian Hall throughout the year from then on with the hall hire at the time being four pound four shillings.

The Warragul YFC organized rallies right across Gippsland and why so many young people attended the rallies or responded to the message and activities YFC brought may be contentious. The message by today's standards may have been conservative yet the activities were certainly not. What YFC offered was a form of what Theodore Roosevelt might describe as 'the brilliance of liberty': i.e. the liberty found in both 'having a go' and knowing when to say 'no'. This was a type of liberty that was inherently adventurous and courageous while remaining virtuous. The goal was not to just walk toward something, but give courage to walk away from 'stuff': the stuff that would hinder the eternal goal. Through YFC, young people found the courage to say 'no' to the things that hurt themselves and others.

The Mud Bowl

This was a youth organisation on the cutting edge in the 1960's and the local Warragul leaders copped quite a bit of criticism for their rather risqué teen attracting activities. One of those popular activities was the 'Mud Bowl' held on Rowse's farm.

The YFC didn't only prepare the spiritual soil for the hungry teens but spent a few days preparing the natural environment. A paddock of rich red soil was ploughed up and drenched with water literally creating an acre sized mud bowl. Frolicking in the mud, having 'flour fights' and being hosed down by the local Fire Brigade offered a pretty good illustration of the human condition and was mountains of fun for all. The activity attracted busloads of young people from Melbourne, up to 400 at a time aged between 12-20. They arrived with lots of enthusiasm and a change of clothes. The activity also attracted truckloads of criticism. But the results spoke for themselves.

After the Mud Bowl, everyone went to 'the shed', i.e. Rowse's flower shed, for the evening message. Not only were many lifetime friendships created and prodigal sons restored, the flower shed and other YFC activities provided opportunity for many blooming romances.

That Mud Bowl was good clean fun for all.

YFC was all about empowering young people to reach other young people and the Warragul chapter had its own Teenage Committee known as 'Teenteam'. They organized meetings that attracted 40-50 youth every fortnight. Frank and Bev Brown, now in their 70s, were the first teen leaders and are among many YFC 'youth' that remain in leadership positions across a wide spectrum of churches throughout Australia. Fifty years on, they are still committed Christians.

In those early days, in addition to the fortnightly 'Insight' Bible Studies, there was a special games night called 'Impact' on the alternate week. Youth would bring their friends to participate in what might be called 'crazy' games. No doubt some of them would be outlawed today for Occupational Health and Safety reasons. But back then the youth loved them.

They also loved the WYFC camps which were also full of fun and games. These started in 1968 at Adanac, Yarra Junction the year after George and Bev were married and within two years WYFC had outgrown their facilities. On the June long weekend in 1970, WYFC had its first camp at Raymond Island and this became a standing booking until 2001 enabling the campers to increase from 40 to 120. This time it was the Rowse's flower truck that was central to the success of the camp. It left Warragul Post Office at 6am stuffed with all the campers bedding, clothes, food and camping supplies and was a feature of the camp. In the final years, the Jindi truck was used.

Raymond Island is just 200m off the coast, across from the town of Paynesville and is approximately 6 km long by 2 km wide. Here the campers met in big A-Frame community buildings with a bunkhouse for the boys that by all accounts 'was on the rough side' with something 'slightly better' for the girls. The only access to the camp was by punt and activities included waterskiing and earth ball. George didn't think earth ball would be a permissible game today. A soft air filled ball 5 foot (or 1.5M) in diameter provided a fun ride with the kids being rolled around on it. But it also provided quite a falling distance to the hard earth below. Not content with that level of risk, some got the idea of perching Jenny (and other smaller campers) on the top of the ball with two of the bigger ones taking a 20metre run up into either side of it catapulting the smaller child into the air. That was, until George saw it. Despite no real accidents, some managed to rise as much as 10 feet (3M) into the air! One day Jenny and Narelle rushed in to report that earth ball was no longer on earth having blown out across the lake. An exhilarating expedition in the boat was mounted to retrieve earth ball but sadly, retrieval required stabbing it.

One of the other experiences campers loved was literally electrifying. It was an electric chair that came out from America and was popular at the YFC camps in the very early days. The chair was just a wooden stool with a bit of square wire mesh on top. Underneath the stool was a T-Model Ford Trembler Coil with its own 9 Volt battery. As the story goes, it was set up "so that if you sat on it, and somebody else activated it, it felt like a million pricks on your backside." Touching it with a knife would give the young people the excitement of seeing sparks jump around but what they really preferred were games where they'd see their friends jumping around. The quiz was popular with a contestant on the chair and another in control of the button to give them a 'buzz' for the wrong answer. George recalled that some thought of outsmarting the device and stopping the shock by using silver paper; but they got that terribly wrong! Those who put books down their pants made the better choice.

One of the most popular games with the youth was called Blind Man's Woomp. It was a similar game to the still popular piñata party game but with the potential for that extra buzz! The person on the chair was blindfolded but armed for defense purposes with a rolled *Weekly Times*. The blindfolded person sat with legs apart and the button positioned between their legs. The object of the game was to use the Weekly Times, flaying backward and forward, to clobber the attacker on the head and stop them from reaching the button between their legs and administering a zap.

This wasn't an ordeal the leaders were unprepared to test themselves. The Melbourne YFC had the chair first and the Warragul leaders then requested one too. The first-time George and Wally tested the chair was at a board meeting and none of the board members had ever seen anything like it. Laurie Morley was persuaded to sit on it first providing a lot of entertainment for the others as he flew one way and the chair another. In a playful way, the chair was also used as a deterrent for bad behavior at the camps but the kids seemed to love it even doing silly things so they could be zapped. Wally said it was a similar strength to an electric fence and you could adjust it. They all loved the countdown …10, 9, 8 … as they waited for the shock. (They still have the chair and it still works well, but has little use!)

Being the cold month of June, one of the first things George and Wally attended to at the Raymond Island campsite was to put 'Sally' in her place. Sally was a 6-foot (1.8 metre) diesel fired heater and she provided a warm central place in the extremely high A-Frame building to gather around for meals, singing and Bible messages. Sally sat in her own big tub or barrel to which the diesel was added and from this her chimney extended upward; an arrangement that should really have only be used in open air areas or very big sheds. But as George would say, "when the campers gathered around Sally it meant we were going to have a really good time together." Sally had her own moods and to the campers' delight would sometimes 'blow her stack' with flames leaping from the top and smoke billowing on the ceiling. When she was really hot, Sally glowed red around the belly. She not only maintained a warm temperature but an atmosphere suitable for indoor fun and games.

One of those much-loved games was potentially suffocating. A tunnel was created from heavy black plastic and a team of young men were positioned at one end with a team of young women at the other. There was great excitement to see who could crawl through to be first at the other's end. Being black it was extremely dark inside the makeshift plastic tunnel and the inevitable entanglement as runners passed each other offered plenty of amusement. In the awkward scramble to victory, head butting was often unavoidable but the only real side effect suffered from this rather risqué game was a dose of 'the stitch' from all the laughter.

Putting their Christianity in practice, the campers seemed willing to suffer a few uncomfortable experiences in order to help others. Sponsored eat-a-thons were organized for the needy in India. The aim of this activity was to see who could eat the most of any one food leaving a few enthusiasts reaching for the bucket. Wally Kenney's son managed to take the prize for downing 85 cocktail frankfurters in one sitting. One year it was ice-cream and another year porridge, but whatever that food was, the goal of raising lots of money was achieved with the added bonus of fun memories for all. No doubt the campers learnt a few lessons in overdoing it as well!

The YFC coin-a-thin was a novel way to put fun into giving an offering. Two teams would compete to make the longest line of end-on-end coins. This meant the campers would dig a little deeper in their pockets to win and the fundraising effort benefited from the competitiveness.

There were no shortage of practical jokers, pranks or mischievous games at the camps. George and Bev recall one evening at the dinner table. Jenny and fellow camper Josh Coates had been faking illness all day and halfway through their dinner they said they felt sick and grabbed their tummies. Unbeknown to all but a few, they had hot water bottles filled with vegetable soup under their tops and as they grabbed their tummies and squeezed them, this caused the soup to spill out like vomit. To the horror of most, the few in on the joke began eating 'the vomit' commenting how nice it was.

The Leaders Hunt was another popular activity. About six YFC leaders would disguise themselves and catch the punt across to Paynesville. Blending in to the environment as a local window cleaner, shopper or whatever they could imagine to be, enabled them to remain incognito. The campers would then be released with the challenge of finding and identifying the leaders. George's son-in-law Glen once disguised himself as an old lady in a wheelchair so effectively the team couldn't spot him anywhere. At one stage, he had another person push him across the road and deliberately run him into the curb so he would fall out. People came running to help but he still wasn't recognized. One other leader buried himself in the sand while another dressed up as a drunk vagrant and was so authentic he was reported to Police!

"When discipline was fun you had a good camp" … George

Discipline could be fun. Because extra help was needed for the final clean up, YFC played Camp Cop. The cop would *dob in* campers for misdemeanours and the final day of reckoning was complete with court, judge and jury. Campers would discover they'd been caught out and booked for silly things with penalties including toilet cleaning and other less desirable tasks. This created a special interest in solving the mystery of who the Camp Cop actually was.

Camp discipline was very different to a disciplined home life. It was the norm at this time for most students to have a pretty regimented earlier bed time but at the YFC camp an effort was made to keep everyone occupied with games until about 11pm. This would ensure campers were all pretty tired. Realizing they had to rise for the compulsory 7am 'Rise and Shine' exercises, it was hoped they wouldn't want to waste too much shut eye time between. 'Rise and Shine' was set to music and came to be more realistically known as 'Moan and Groan'. Sleeping through 'Moan and Groan' and failure to get breakfast could risk the electric chair. George and Bev's youngest child Shelley wasn't old enough to be a camper but her role from five years of age was to provide the 'wakey-wakey' call on the megaphone and the 13-25 year olds were much more affable toward young Shelley.

One thing everyone agreed on about YFC camps was the quality of the speakers. The youth always listened attentively and for all the daily frivolity, the biblical messages were taken seriously. At these camps, young people continued to make their commitment to Jesus as their personal Lord. Everyone understood the camps were faith based and the youth wanted to attend them because they were well organized, lots of fun, meaningful and life changing. And nothing was really stock and standard. YFC even had special bright red Bibles made for the youth.

George, Bev, Wally and many other YFC leaders and helpers dedicated their lives to offer youth these unique camping experiences. For 25 years over the first weekend in December, George and Wally also took 15-25 year olds to Licola on a 4WD camping adventure.

Licola is located 248kms east of Melbourne on the Wellington River and provided a great spot for youth to get in touch with God, themselves, nature and others. Like all the camps, there was a focus on both practical life skills and spirituality. The youth brought their own food and were responsible for cooking it. For some of them it was the first time they had ever had to take care of themselves. Many discovered the hard way not to leave food out overnight. In the cool evenings as they sat around the campfire sharing their stories, many would ask "what's all this Jesus stuff about…" The Licola bush became a place where genuine desire to understand the meaning of life was birthed.

Life in the bush was totally different and even the Park Ranger would overlook some of the rules that would normally apply. There were times he spotted the Toyota tray tops with kids packed in, standing on the frame on the back or sitting on the bull bar across the front. They all wanted to sit on the bull bar to experience the splash as George and Wally accelerated out of the rivers. The Park Ranger did pull George up one day but just said "be careful going on the road with them won't you!"

The kids learnt how to live in the bush and went canoeing and hiking. One of the features of the Licola bush camp was a trip up to Mt Margaret to play a game that resembled a wild form of bowls. The 'bowling ball' was a big rock thrust over the very steep cliff and the object was to see how many trees you could hit as the rock made its way down. But it wasn't all rough and tumble and boyish stuff. George recalls one of the girls, who happened to be a hairdresser, giving him a head massage in the middle of the river. There was a place for everyone.

Today parents and youth hold different concerns to those in the

1960 – 1990's and some might be concerned about YFC methods. A fitting YFC Motto may be worth noting:

Anchored to the Rock

Geared to the Times

Our methods change, our message never changes

No doubt some of those methods have had their day.

George has kept this clipping from June 1994 among his personal treasures reflecting both his sense of humour and the seismic scale of the cultural shift since BV: i.e. Before video recorders (some will now ask – what are they?).

Newspaper article 25th June 1994

The YFC activities always went beyond the camps to offer other special experiences for kids throughout the year. The Melbourne chapter organised a city hay ride down Bourke Street enlisting 20 Coca Cola flatbed trucks which they covered with hay bales and kids. The Warragul chapter organized a special 'banana split'. The split was housed in a length of roof spouting 30-40 feet long (9-12 metres). George and Wally filled the roof spouting with bananas and ice-cream and lined up 200-300 youth, armed only with spoons and an appetite to eat as much as they could. A lot of time went into organizing fun youth programs that attracted the locals. Yet the whole purpose of these fun activities was not just to have fun, but to give youth an opportunity to think about life, eternity and the choices they would make.

The YFC was an organization that connected Christian youth leaders globally. George and Bev's first International Convocation, and Bev's first flight, was in 1984 to Hong Kong. Their youngest child Shelley was only 8 months old and so it was somewhat of a sacrifice to make the trip. But what this trip provided was the bigger YFC picture. George, Bev, Wally and others may have led camps to isolated parts of Victoria but WYFC members really weren't isolated. They were part of a worldwide youth movement changing thousands of young lives by making faith real and fun. George and Bev continue to support this International Ministry. In recent years at a Denmark Convocation, some YFC speakers' names had to be suppressed. Indicative of the times we live in, some speakers couldn't even talk about their activities in their own countries. It's clear in a number of ways, the brilliance of liberty once enjoyed is fading.

Yet, the YFC does still operate in 112 nations and globally has 51,000 full time volunteer staff. It is still strong in Brazil. George recalls

50,000 Brazilian mothers praying for the ministry and incredible things happening there. The impact of YFC around the globe and locally cannot be overstated. Victoria hosted many American teams in those early days. There were Teenteam concerts, sheepstakes and pig roasts at Mill Valley Ranch catering for up to 600 youth at a time. Many Victorian musicians had their musical careers kick started as a result of YFC talent quests. There were huge youth festivals at Belgrave Heights every March and September called 'Youth Happening'. At one Youth Happening, American Soul Star, Tommy Tipton, exuding his powerful personal presence over 3,000 youth, moved them to quiet tears with that classic old song 'Jesus Loves Me'. The message really hit the spot.

There were endless YFC meetings for the faithful. George and Bev were conduits of all they absorbed at those international leadership meetings hosting fortnightly LUG group meetings in their own home. LUG was an acronym for *Leaders Under Guidance* however was locally understood as *Leaders Under George!* For over 10 years, there were up to a dozen young leaders attending these fortnightly meetings at the Ronalds' home incorporating Bible study, prayer, strategy and planning for camps, youth meetings and other activities.

Perhaps YFC was so popular because at this time, churches had yet to develop their own youth ministries. And at this time, schools welcomed Christian programs giving brilliant YFC musicians the opportunity to perform to school assemblies. George acknowledges the musicians would use appropriate material for a school assembly, but stresses they were not shy in presenting a strong message to gear their youthful audience toward a Saturday rally. Some may recall the American band *Carpenters Tools* which was well known among

Australian schools. One of the most popular Australian bands was *Travellers* organized and run by Alan & Mavis Peterson of Sydney. Music and school visits were a vital part of the YFC ministry and in this era, churches were right behind them.

George and Bev, with young children in tow, all attended the Warragul Community Church where George was an elder for 25 years. Today, with Andrew and wife Catriona, Jenny and husband Glen, they have the joy of still attending Warragul Community Church with some of their grandchildren.

The Warragul chapter of YFC made enormous contributions to the lives of Victorian youth and notably achieved this through generous volunteerism. Six other Victorian chapters folded, but Warragul YFC continues to this day. Until recently, it was supported by Denise Spink who started in the mid 1980's as the first full time worker. George recalls teaching Denise in Sunday School. She always referred to him as her favorite teacher and as George jokes, "she never wanted to get out of my class." In a way, it appears she didn't. George stepped aside as the WYFC Director after 26 years and, until recently, his niece Chris Hobbs continued to run the Warragul chapter. Like an Olympic torch, the Warragul lamp keeps burning.

Leaders Hunt, Raymond Island YFC Camp

The Earthball at YFC Raymond Island Camp

Meal time, YFC Raymond Island Camp

YFC Licole 4WD Camp

YFC Mudbowl

6
The blokes, the bush, the bravado

2017-2018 A Golden Quinquagenarian Age

The year 2017 was significant in George and Bev's life marking 50 years of their shared life as husband and wife. This 50-year union has successfully incorporated care not just for each other, but has included so many others.

George's quinquagenarian loves include, but are not limited to, a Land Rover he purchased the same year he married and the annual 4WD bush trips they've shared that have attracted 'youths' spanning those 50 years. Some of those eternal youths are still going bush with George 50 years on. These adventure-seeking grandpas continue to head for the high country with kids and grandkids in tow, passing on the opportunity for them to learn how to live in the bush. 4WD yarns are threaded through George and Bev's shared life but deep in the Australian bush, it was his best mate and navigator Wally, right there by his side.

The year 1968 ushered in the inaugural bush trip for George and his beloved Land Rover and gave Harry Scouller the opportunity to put his newly purchased defence vehicle to the test. Harry had bought an ex-army 4WD Austin Champ with a 5-speed gearbox complete with forward and reverse levers. This enabled the Champ to go backwards at the same speed it went forwards making for an awful lot of high-speed bush fun whatever the direction.

This first bush trip was to Lake Tali Karng which is known as the 'hidden lake' because it's nestled between hills high up in the Victorian Alps. In the 1960s there was access for 4WD enthusiasts via a steep, rugged and challenging track about 30km from Licola. The track offered 23 crossings through Wellington River enabling George and his co-adventurers to 4WD within a few hundred metres of the lake. Designated in later years as a sacred place to the Gunaikurnai people, it is now only accessible by foot and no camping is permitted at the lake itself.

The following year George and his Land Rover made the trip to Lake Tali Karng with David Rowse and the 'posse' they inspired who were on 100cc farm bikes and 90cc Postie step through bikes. The river crossings were especially challenging and compared to today's standards, the riding tracks and vehicle suspension were very rough. There was less emphasis on safety clothing (and safety in general) so most bikers opted for overalls and everyday gumboots. Those who could afford it had a helmet.

It was 1970 when the explorers ventured further north making the first of many trips to Wonnangatta Station; Peter Rowse in his Toyota tray top, George and Wally in the Land Rover, Robin Pocklington and Laurie Morley both riding Postie bikes, with David Rowse on a 100cc Yamaha bike. They loved the thrill and adventure in finding natures hidden treasures and Wonnangatta Station didn't disappoint.

The Station is hidden within the Alpine National Park about three hours north-west of Dargo. The Parks Victoria website describes the area as a remote and rugged haven for wildlife with grand scenery and wonderful wildflowers. The station enjoys typically cool evenings lending itself to gatherings around a camp fire while catching a sense of Australian history. This is an area where cattle grazing had its beginnings and it was once the home of the pioneering Bryce family. The station ruins hold added mystery being the site of an old unsolved double murder, no doubt sparking a few other campfire stories.

Going bush always gave opportunity for the men to show mateship. One such opportunity arose heading up the rough, steep track to Howitt Hut from Wonnangatta Station. Peter had run out of power requiring George to pull him up the hill. In subsequent years when his clutch was slipping, it was George who needed to be pushed over the hills giving Peter the opportunity to return the favour. Even as grandpa's, these men have never been too far 'over the hill' to help one another.

It was their practice to camp the night on a river and also their practice to gather together for a time of devotion on Sunday mornings. George still has a vivid recollection of Robin Pocklington's message on this occasion which offered a reflection of the Biblical story of Jesus riding into Jerusalem on a donkey. He also recalls his own thoughts at the time. "If the Lord could use a donkey, perhaps he could use a donkey like me!" The men used Billy Tea as substitute communion wine giving this ancient bonding ritual a truly Australian flavor.

When they arrived at the station, the men saw it was in good shape with the cattle keeping it all clean. Behind the remnants of the old homestead was a track up a very steep hill which was aptly named the Widow Maker. To these adventurers, the Widow Maker was too good a challenge to be ignored. Making it to the top was an exhilarating opportunity to test the skills of bike and rider. But when visiting the site in more recent years, the men discovered a 'Road Closed' sign at the bottom of the track. Not to be deterred, Peter raced up anyway repeating history with his successful ascent. It seemed like a good plan going up but what Peter didn't plan on was being met by two DSE officers (Department of Sustainability and Environment) on the way down. Apparently, they had a poor sense of humour and Peter was fined $200 for his misadventure. He later confessed that was one of the best $200 he had ever spent.

In succeeding years 'The Bush Trip' attracted men and their sons from across Victoria. On the earlier bush trips, there were up to 25 motor bikes plus several other vehicles but the mix of bikes and 4WDs altered in later years. More recently George's bush motorcade has included 25-30 4WD vehicles and 10-12 bikes with details of the trips relying solely on the 'bush telegraph'. There is no official advertising, yet enthusiasts just seem to hear about the upcoming Bush Trip.

George and David Rowse initially took on the responsibility of planning these annual trips. They had good forest maps and obtained advice from Forestry Authorities to ensure the tracks they were planning to use were open. Camp sites in focus had to be along a river with access to plenty of fresh water and somewhere to wash or swim. This could be anywhere between Omeo and Marysville. Jamieson was slightly north of these end points but offered plenty of good bush tracks. 'Good' in bush vernacular meant challenging.

In the early years, many tracks in the high country were rough and poorly maintained with patches that were washed out and boggy; getting bogged was par for the course. The thrill of river crossings often included rescuing a drowning bike which sometimes couldn't be repaired so would end up on the back of a 4WD.

And then there were the antics inspired by the untamed bush environment. Harry Scouller's Austin Champ wasn't just famous because it could go backwards at the same speed it went forwards. The Champ had a waterproof Rolls Royce engine which naturally screamed to these bushmen to be tested and they decided to try it out in the Wongungura River near Dargo. With the roof folded down, Harry and his mate Ian Coates, who was also Bev's cousin, drove into the river. George and the others watched from the bank as the vehicle was totally immersed. All that remained protruding above the water were Harry and Ian's head and shoulders and the snorkel they had positioned to give the motor some air. Bubbles were flowing from the exhaust as the sound of bubbling laughter began to fill the air. Harry and Ian had forgotten to take out their food box and bedding which were now floating downstream. This only added to the men's delight. All were witnesses to Champ's waterproof claims. As George tells the story "the Austin Champ would keep on going in that river as long as the snorkel was above the water."

Sometimes it was just too long between annual excursions and a special day trip was called to quench the men's thirst for adventure. With its many steep tracks dating back to the gold fever days, Walhalla was always a good destination. It was also popular with George and Wally because it was only a little over an hour away from Jindivick. The first time they attempted this particular track with a couple of other 4WDrivers, they were in the Land Rover at the rear of a convoy of 10 bikes. George and Wally could hear the bikes working hard in front but until they came around a corner, had no vision to see what the noise was all about. As they took the corner, and the blue haze created from the 2-stroke smoke parted, they were faced with an incredibly steep hill standing in defiance of the men attempting to navigate it. Either side of the track bikes were lying on their side while others were being manually pushed up the hill by their defeated riders. Not deterred, George decided he'd have a go in the Land Rover and taking it as steady as he could, he launched ahead. About half way up as they were bouncing over rocks there was an almighty bang from the back of their vehicle. It was immediately obvious the Land Rover had a broken axle and fortunate its owner had imbibed the Boy Scout motto; Be Prepared. Prepared they were, having carried a spare. The vehicle was winched onto a tree and secured with extra ropes, before jacking up the back. Fortuitously, one of the men had a felt hat which in the absence of alternatives he sacrificially offered as a vessel to drain the oil into. The hat held up well for the task at hand, though was undoubtedly unfit for its primary function after this. Within an hour, the crew were on their way again and that defiant hill became known as 'Axle Hill'.

In 1995 George bought his first Land Rover Defender, which he confidently asserts is a much more capable vehicle for bush bravado. This would be the first of three Defenders he'd invest in.

David moved to Queensland around 2003 with George continuing to plan the annual bush excursions which became known as 'George's bush weekend'. George liked to secure the site for the weekend on the Wednesday prior and generally did this with his brother Alan, Wally and 4-5 other enthusiasts who were up for an extra-long weekend. He always found this time very special; especially those times around the campfire when the stars were shining in a clear night sky and all being men of faith, they could reflect on the deeper meaning of life together. Leading up to the weekend, George would make 3-4 phone calls to advise where they were going. As the 'camp securers' sat around that campfire earlier in the week, they waited to see who might turn up. The 'bush telegraph' worked effectively and most arrived in groups settling in around their own campfires. Many new friendships were made each year while others were renewed.

Saturday was planned as the adventure day when they all headed off to tackle some challenging track and river crossing. This was often in two groups due to the sheer number of 4WD vehicles. In recent years George led one group with his nephew Steve Ronalds leading the other. The bikes would travel separately but the planning included a place for all to meet together for lunch. The campfires scattered around the site on Saturday evening made a perfect setting for all the good-humored stories. Laughter filled the night air and George recalls comments from some who had experience in 4WD clubs. They just couldn't believe these adventurers could have so much fun without grog and coarse jokes. It was generally accepted there wasn't any alcohol but as George says "we all knew some of the men had some and no one was condemning. We all had a lot of fun."

This was the perfect environment for many men to open up. On the Sunday morning, each brought his own camp chair to form a large circle around the fire and one by one they would say who they were and where they came from. Then someone always brought a challenging message from the Bible. Having never stepped into a church, this was the only opportunity some of them had to intersect with faith and in this very real and rugged environment, with very real and rugged friends, it was indeed a safe space to give consideration to weightier matters. Robin Pocklington is still one of the regular speakers.

George has seen a lot of change over the years. Those rugged old tracks are now kept in much better order and some more hazardous tracks have been closed. Vehicles have improved suspension and braking and a lot have anti-lock/anti-skid braking systems (ABS) and traction controls fitted with more powerful and efficient motors. It's a different era. There were once no licenses required for farm bikes; life gave you license.

Now past his 80th birthday, George still drives a late model Defender and loves it. Recent trips with his brother, come navigator, Alan and son Andrew, have included up to 90 other men. Sadly, his constant companion Wally's health issues began restricting his twilight years' bush adventures. Nevertheless, some of the drivers still 4WD'ing with George have been doing so for 20-30 years and now bring their grandsons. It's all a pretty big deal and makes for a large camp site. George laments that most large sites are now comparatively civilized; they are mowed and even have the luxury of drop toilets. This is a far cry from the challenging type of camping these older men were used to.

Reflections of a once in lifetime adventure: Crossing the Simpson Desert

The Simpson Desert is the largest expanse of parallel sand dunes in the world and crossing it has been described as a once in a life time adventure. When Laurie Morley suggested they should do it, it came as no surprise to anyone that George and Wally didn't ask why, but why not!

The Simpson Desert track straddles three states, the Northern Territory, South Australia and Queensland. It starts in Birdsville

(Outback Queensland) and runs across the top of South Australia to Dalhousie Springs, and onto Mt Dare. The 550km expedition requires negotiating 1100 sand dunes and depending on weather conditions, it normally takes about 4-5 days to make the crossing. But as there's no food, fuel or water to be found crossing this great expanse, travelers need to take sufficient supplies for 10 days in case of an emergency. And as good Boy Scouts, when George and Wally set off in the year 2000, they were well prepared.

Their Simpson Desert trip was launched from Birdsville, which offered the last place for the three vehicles to refresh and refuel after the rough journey on the corrugated road. George and Wally were in the Defender, Laurie drove his 80 series Toyota Landcruiser, and Laurie's friends Ben and Jenny were in their Nissan Navara. Having enjoyed a good meal and peaceful sleep at the rather famous Birdsville Pub, early the next day they put civilization behind them in a cloud of dust.

Looming in the distance stood Big Red. At 40-50 metres, this monumental sand dune was a sight to behold. It's the first and biggest of the sand dunes to cross ex-Birdsville and is appropriately named Big Red due to the rusting iron particles in the sand. Big Red is not easily conquered and challenges many 4WD enthusiasts. Laurie was to be among them and was very frustrated that Big Red got the better of his old Toyota and wouldn't allow him to ascend. The Defender did make it up and from here George could relish the incredible view. To the west he saw the track winding up and down over the sand dunes until it finally disappeared somewhere into the distance.

Later that morning the convoy arrived at Eyre Creek crossing to discover heavy rainfall had left it impassable. It was simply too deep and they had to go 30kms upstream to a shallower crossing before returning to the track. By mid-afternoon a suitable camp site had been located and they settled in.

George recalls with amazement the stillness of the desert; it's absolute silence. This was particularly notable as they sat around the evening campfire watching the light from the fire flicker on the surrounding trees and tents. The brightness of the stars reached down to the horizon giving them a humbling sense of perspective regarding their own significance in God's vast creation. Occasionally the silence would be broken by the howl of a dingo or sometimes they would hear a wild donkey bray. The silence wasn't uncomfortable. George will tell you "I don't know of anyone else who has been a mate like Wally and I have been for each other. We share anything together." But sharing doesn't necessarily mean words. On one 2 ½ hour trip to go fishing in Bairnsdale, George recalls that he and Wally would have talked for only 5 minutes. But the time, the silence, was very special. Like their quinquagenarian friendship, silence was golden. As George said "we are just enjoying each other's company." Perhaps enjoying the silence with someone else is another lost art.

The next morning the adventurers headed west to Poeppel Corner where Queensland, Northern Territory, and South Australia intersect. The point is named after Augustus Poeppel, who conducted a survey in the 1880s to exactly mark out the borders of the three central states with a coolibah post he had dragged there by camel. The post has since moved to more accurately reflect the intersection and was even replaced in 1989, while an official marker has been laid to definitively mark today's state borders nearby. [12]

The ups and downs of the next day included countless sand dunes with each one offering its own challenge. They also crossed the

---

[12] "Hema - Hay River Track to Poeppel Corner", https://cloud.hemaexplorer.com.au

occasional dry salt plain and spotted a few wild camels. But what they were always on the lookout for as they ascended the sand dune was any on coming vehicles. Desert protocol mandates that all vehicles fly a red flag 2 meters high from the front of their 4WD in order to remain visible to oncoming vehicles while approaching the crest of a sand dune.

The third day offered more sand dunes, low scrub and a few stunted trees. But as a very dramatic sky began to over-shadow the landscape, the group knew this wasn't going to be a 'more of the same' kind of day. Having seen the storm rise right in front of them, they made camp early and it was just as well. By 4-5 o'clock the sun had completely disappeared behind those ink black storm clouds rising in the west. Streaks of lightning then lit up the sky and this was followed by thunder. It was a menacing sight.

George parked the Defender next to their tent in an attempt to shelter it from the impact of the impending storm and expected onslaught of torrential rain and wind. The wind began to blow so hard that George and Wally thought the best way to hold down their small 2-man tepee was to sit on their beds inside it. Completely outsized and surrounded by darkness, their vulnerability was tangible. But after an hour or so, the storm passed as quickly as it had come. And as it receded into the distance, all that was left hanging over the desert was an eerie quietness. When George surveyed the campsite, he saw that Ben and Jenny had taken refuge in their Nissan and Laurie and his mates were all OK too. But nobody got much sleep that night.

The next morning after the rain, everything was pristine and clean. The rain had firmed the track down. Being minus the dust, it was much better 4WD'ing and within an hour they were cresting another sand dune. From here they could see what looked like water shimmering in the distance and realized as they got closer that the downpour had left the salt plains awash, obscuring the tracks. So, they walked into the shallow water where the track seemed to be firm and about 300 metres across got a siting of the track on the other side of the flooded plain. George slowly edged the Defender in and made it over, and the others successfully followed. There were several more salt lakes to navigate that day, lots of mud and many more sand dunes before pitching their tents for the night at Purni Bore. This artificial bore on the threshold of the Simpson has created a wetland busy with birdlife and still produces lots of hot water. The only interruption to a sound nights' sleep for the weary travelers at Purni Bore, was the sound of a braying donkey walking between their tents.

With the 1140 sand dunes behind them, they were now faced with the comparatively easy track into Dalhousie Springs for a well-earned dip in the thermal pools. Dalhousie Springs is a group of over 60 natural artesian springs located in Witjira National Park on the western fringe of the Simpson Desert, 180km northeast of Oodnadatta in northern South Australia. The only service available within the Witjira National Park and the Simpson Desert Conservation Park is offered by Mt Dare Hotel and hence, after refueling the plan was to head off to Oodnadatta. They were advised not to waste any time as another storm was brewing which was expected to hit late afternoon. Having called ahead to book rooms at the caravan park, they set off.

About half way, George went through a dry creek bed and as he changed gears, he lost his drive completely. Marooned, he radioed Laurie. "Something's gone wrong, I've got no gears, no nothing, no drive!" He found out later the centre of the clutch had failed. Laurie came back and the group prayed about what to do deciding they would keep on going. A snatch strap was hooked on to Laurie's Land

Cruiser and they set of in tow, which is most embarrassing for a Land Rover owner. It was, however, a proud moment for Laurie who made sure George wouldn't live down being towed by his Toyota.

George will causally mention that a snatch strap "has a fair bit of elasticity." For the uninitiated, a snatch strap upon failure, can break windows, dent panels or take out eyes. With the Defender's motor idling to facilitate steering and braking, George found it difficult to keep tension on the rope. What's more, the storm was approaching and they were still about an hour out of Oodnadatta. When the storm hit them, it turned the road to mud within 5 minutes. Now George had red mud being plastered over the windscreen further obscuring his vision. He and Laurie kept communication open via the radio and as expected, they soldiered on.

Darkness set in about 15kms out of Oodnadatta and as they were crossing a salt plain George and Wally felt a bit of a bump and heard a bang. George radioed Laurie commenting how the road was very corrugated to which Laurie replied "No – I don't think so." George mentioned to Wally that they seemed to be getting closer to Laurie and Wally opened his door a little to check it out. He heard something dragging but they just kept going.

It was a welcome sight to see lights ahead and the thought of a dry room was inviting. The caravan park owners, understandably concerned for their safety, were very relieved to see the latecomers join Ben and Jenny who had arrived earlier. The next morning the Police came to make sure they were OK and told the group both roads out of Oodnadatta were closed and would remain so for a number of days.

In the stark light of day, the vehicles all covered in red mud looked a sorry sight and the source of the mysterious bump, bang and drag was able to be identified. In the darkness, George had run over the snatch strap and it had wrapped itself around the axle and main steering arm between the wheels and snapped the steering arm. This was what Wally heard dragging.

For the last 15kms they'd only had steering to one wheel, with the other wobbling wildly, and it appeared to be a miracle they were able to keep going at all. George was always assured he was being looked after from above. As soon as they tried to move the Defender the next morning, the wheels turned sideways and remained rigid, not allowing any further movement at all. George was in awe of how they got it there.

As the weather was starting to improve they all decided to have a look around. The main road was underwater and as far as you could see in every direction, it was flooded. So much so, that the next day 4 American girls in bikinis captured everyone's attention when they found a canoe and were trying to row it up the Main Street. The famous Oodnadatta Pink Roadhouse was still open for business, and the only other business in town was the local garage. That's where they headed. Flood waters had also marooned the local mechanic somewhere between his garage and Adelaide leaving his offsider to handle the business. Having explained the problem, they went back to the Defender, took the steering arm off and took it down to the garage to weld it up themselves. While there, George noticed an A-Frame hanging on the wall (a steel frame in the shape of an A. The point end has a tow bar coupling and the other two ends are able to hook on to a bull bar). This was just what they needed and the young man in the garage said they could have it if they dropped it back on their next trip. Only in the country!

After 4 nights, the Police finally opened the road to Maree. It was goodbye to maddening mud and hello to beautiful bitumen. Having adapted the A-Frame to fit, the innovative explorers embarked on the long, slow 1500km journey home. It was, and wasn't, the most interesting trip home given George and Wally could sit there with arms folded knowing the Defender would automatically follow Laurie's vehicle. All they could see for 1500kms was the distance to the window in front of them. One young man at a petrol station en-route commented "gee – that's a good way to save fuel" to which George replied "yes, it makes it very economical!" When they entered the state of Victoria, they went to the 'Cop Station' to see if it was legal to tow like they were. The local guy didn't know so he rang Melbourne to check it out. They didn't know either, so they just kept going. George was forever grateful to Laurie, who now had the opportunity to rib George as much as he and Wally had been ribbing him! Laurie towed him back to his home which was near Shepparton. Bev met them there and continued towing the Defender the rest of the way home behind her Range Rover. The Oodnadatta garage assistant's faith in their honesty was not misplaced. George's son Andrew returned the A-Frame the following year while he was travelling through in the Defender.

George still loves his 4WD but at 80 years young, some friends are beginning to ask "how long are ya gonna do it for?" To this George replies with a chuckle, "as long as I can hang onto the steering wheel!"

George's 4WD trip

Clay pan Simpson Desert after the rain

Climbing Big Red

Harry Scouller in his Austin Champ

George's 4WD trip

7

Another Pioneering Partnership

Some people associate 1984 with George Orwell's futuristic book by that title but that isn't the association George Ronalds would naturally make. Yet it was a significant year for him and Bev and one in which they launched into unchartered territories. In George's 1984, an opportune thought developed into an enterprising cheese factory. The same year, Bev took her first flight to accompany George to their first YFC International Convocation. And it was 1984 when Paul and Debbie Howells first walked into their small community church meeting in Warragul beginning an association that would greatly impact their future life.

Paul and Debbie were missionaries who were on their way to the Philippines. Warragul may not seem 'on the way' but the opportunity to share with this community put Warragul on their flight plan. It was perfect timing for George and Bev because they had just returned from the YFC International Conference in the Philippines which had sparked their interest in the region. It also gave George the opportunity after the meeting to exercise the one Filipino word he'd learnt, "Salamat Po" which means 'thank you very much.' With their shared pioneering spirit, the two couples had an instant connection.

From this initial brief encounter blossomed a friendship which cemented George's commitment to help Paul and Debbie with their work. He offered what missionaries need most; prayerful, pragmatic and financial support. George's pragmatism ultimately led him to take teams of helpers to the village of Lapoc, on the island of Mindanao to assist with building, teaching and encouraging others. As this was a remote, rather lawless place, where 'an eye for an eye' system of retribution was in operation and inter-clan warfare and murder was common, encouragement was much needed. It was all too easy to lose courage, that is become discouraged, so this type of support could never be underestimated.

Like George and Bev, Paul and Debbie could never be accused of having a dead faith; i.e. faith without action.[13] They exemplified what it means to put faith into action. In Lapoc, this meant providing basic medical aid, a clinic building and also training local medical workers. Paul was a very capable business man and highly resourceful when it came to building, carpentry and electrical installations. Both Paul and Debbie also trained teams around them who later developed their own teams with the ability to work independently in their fields.

This partnership with the Howells also gave George additional opportunity to exercise his own passions. It was a win/win. In those early years, dirt bikes were the only means of accessing the area and later when the roads were widened, it was 4WD territory. Occasionally a Jeepney would make the journey in. This was a local bus-type vehicle. The 4WD environment and objective of the mission met George with the type of challenges he enjoyed most.

Like all George's passions, supporting the work of Paul and Debbie became a family affair. On his first trip to the village of Lapoc October 2002, George was accompanied by his daughter

---

[13] The Letter to James, 2:17

Narelle. They drove the 3-hour trip from the airport in Paul's highly modified Jackaroo which had a Landcruiser undercarriage and diff locks all round. This modification was a necessity in order to navigate the river crossings and bog holes that while challenging to some, delighted George.

George's son in law Glen was next to share the experience sometime in 2004. And in August 2006 it was Shelley, the youngest in the family who got a taste of remote village life in a volatile region. All work and no play is not the Ronalds style and this trip included white water rafting on the Cagayan River. This was despite the challenging cultural environment. Shelley's great photos include snaps of some of the local military on patrol reflecting this side of life on the island.

A third generation of the Ronalds clan stepped out of their comfort zone to experience life in Mindanao in 2013. It was November when George and Bev's first grandson Jaziah (son of Jenny and Glen) travelled with Jenny and Bev to the island. Not to be outdone, Andrew and daughter Madeline, number 2 grandchild followed in April 2015. Although they counted it as a wonderful experience Andrew admits it wasn't quite at a comfort standard that they would return to in a hurry.

George also took three building teams to Mindanao. The first was a team of seven in March 2008 and George's brother Alan was the foreman. They built new missionary housing over a 10-day period using timber cut by chainsaws straight from the bush. It had to be dressed up with a power plane and the locals were very good carpenters. Constructing the housing from raw materials like this and working with the local people was a very rewarding experience for the team.

It was 2 years later, July 2010 when George took the next building team; another 'secret seven.' This time the foreman was Wayne; the son-in law of George's brother Alan. Their mission was to build a church in Tinaytayan.

Wayne was a plasterer by trade. George said "the local carpenters were able to improve his skills in the local environment and teach him a thing or two." It was a very manual process. The building was constructed from handmade bricks and the mortar produced through the slow process of sieving through a pile of gravel from the river bed. This had to be carted in bags to the building approximately 200metres down a dirt track. Plenty of time there for teams, not just mortar, to bond!

The third building team travelled in July 2012. George was accompanied by Paul Anderson, the owner of Integra Homes and a builder in Warragul. Paul took three of his carpenters with some others to build a covered court and stage building for two schools. One was in Lapoc and the other in Lirongan.

George and Paul had a number of things in common and one of those things was a healthy sense of humor. Paul would often sneak chicken heads into the soup bowls of his western guests. Although Paul didn't have a problem eating them this provided quite a culture shock to the unsuspecting visitors!

A local delicacy in the Philippines is called a 'balut' which is a developing duck embryo eaten in the shell. Paul challenged the second young team of builders to an egg eating contest and without hesitation, initiated the challenge by swallowing one whole. Following suit, the young builders found themselves coughing and gagging as they crunched on the beginnings of bones and feathers. Paul hadn't disclosed there were varying degrees of growth in the egg and he had swallowed what was pretty much a yoke compared to what he had served to the team!

George loved to be part of the building teams but couldn't always be physically present. Providing the financial means for them to continue expansion enabled him to continue being a part of what they were doing. In 2004 with his support, Paul's local team were able to build a much-needed hall to house their own growing church. And like most of the projects George undertook or supported, it was big. The hall was the size of a full-sized basketball court with an extra 10 feet around it. Toilets, offices and a kitchen were to the side of the hall and it also had a mezzanine floor. This wasn't built just for church meetings but for the local youth to play sport, for church camps and for other large gatherings. Just recently it accommodated 1300 people attending a Family Camp in Lapoc.

It was also gratifying for George and Bev to see their support fund the building of a bore which provided a fresh water supply for the Lapoc missionary compound, church and local village. An observer might be struck by the integrity George's life displays. There is no discord between his faith and deeds. Not only does George work to see clean natural waters flowing into the community, he has always selflessly worked to see the spiritual living waters flow more freely. To this end, George and Bev have been supporting Paul and Debbie's Bible translation work since 2003. The Howells are painstakingly translating the New Testament into the Talaandig dialect. It's always a slow process to ensure the correct meaning is accurately translated and it is envisaged the complete Talaandig New Testament will be ready to print around Christmas/New Year period 2018 - 2019.

George hasn't just had his own amazing journey from very humble beginnings but has been an integral part of Paul and Debbie's. He has literally seen the road to the village emerge from a rough-road track to having paved access from the main city. The greatest change he's witnessed has been the growth of the community. There have been so many lives changed by the power of the message and example Paul and Debbie bring evident in parents, children, whole family groups and community leaders. Today in this volatile area there are over 30 church communities and 2000-3000 Christians with over 10-12,000 children hearing the Bible message in school. That's quite an achievement!

The greatest identity forging decision

Despite his Christian upbringing and its strong influence in his early life, George vividly recalls a decisive moment when Jesus became his own personal Savior. It was 23 January 1949 and he was only 12 years old. Now 80, this experience is as real today for George as it was then. Those tears he speaks of as he tells his own simple story still well up today; they are tears of incredible gratitude.

> I was at home up here and we went to the Gospel Chapel at night 3-4kms up the road in Rokeby, to the monthly Sunday evening service. I had a strict Christian upbringing. Mr Hugh McNiley was the speaker this night and he was staying at our place (we often had speakers stay at our place) and that night he came into my room and bedside and asked me if I had ever accepted Jesus as my Savior. I stammered a bit as I thought 'have I or haven't I?'

> He asked 'would you like to?' and I said 'yes' and I remember kneeling down with tears in my eyes asking the Lord Jesus into my heart and its as plain now as it was then.

George gratefully attributes the direction his life has taken and his successes to the decision he made in this one decisive moment. To this he attributes his peace, identity and hope for the future. This one short conversation brought a deep conviction in 1949 and cemented his boyish faith, his moral code and sorted out his life priorities. While only 15 himself, he was empowered to step up to help other young people make sense of their life. This seemed perfectly natural for George and just an expression of who he was. He always dived into life wholeheartedly. Today George's home faces the creek on his property where he and brother Dave were baptised with his life-time friend Peter Rowse. Given the impact it had, having this moment constantly before his eyes seems appropriate.

Extract from George's address to CPA Meeting
23 September 2004

As I look over my life's journey, the greatest privilege my wife and I had, from a worldly point of view, was to walk up onto the podium in 2002, to a standing ovation at Madison in Wisconsin in front of 600 cheesemakers and politicians (to receive the trophy for World Champion Cheese) and be able to respond and thank those responsible and to quote a verse from the Bible which hangs on my office wall: Jeremiah 33:3 "Call unto me and I will answer you"

I want to tell you, the accolades of this world will count for nothing when I finish my life's journey and see my Saviour's face: the One who died for me back in old Jerusalem 2,000 years ago.

Paul and Debbie Howell *Building project*

Completed church building at Lapoc *School building project*

Team entertaining the local children *One of the Philippines building team*

EPILOGUE
A summing up by George

I feel very privileged to have grown up in a time where we were able to do things without all the regulations and restrictions that are placed on people and businesses today. While education is a privilege and an advantage, I hope 'George from Jindivick' encourages young Australians that you don't have to be a university graduate to make your way through this world. All you need is a good idea, followed by action and an ongoing commitment to hard work, and much can be achieved.

Jindi Cheese gave our family the opportunity to meet some high-profile people over the years and also to be treated as one on occasions. But whether accepting awards on the world stage or back on the farm doing the 'dirty work,' I never really felt any more high-profile. I think we are all just ordinary people struggling to work out who we are and where we belong in this world and firmly believe that regardless of who you are, we are all equal in God's eyes.

When you spend a major chunk of your life as part of something, I don't believe you ever lose the passion for it. I will always have a heart for young people and the work of YFC. I can't imagine not supporting their vision to reach every young person with the message of Christ.

It's great to be able to look back over 50 years of bush trips with the prospect of continuing that avenue of enjoyment with my son, son-in-law's and grandsons. And my emotions still run high when I think about, or share, the reality of the 2009 bush fires. Nothing is a greater reminder of the frailty of life than sitting in a house surrounded by fire aware that your life can be taken at any time. Now that I've past the 80-year milestone, the thing that strikes me most is the brevity of life. I encourage all not to neglect it and treat it as a rehearsal for something else. I'm convinced the decisions we make here on earth will determine where we spend eternity.

Family Update

Bev and I were privileged to have four very capable children; Andrew, Jenny, Narelle and Shelley.

Andrew has 2 daughters, Madeline (b.2005) and Arabella (b.2007), and lives in Warragul with his loving wife Catriona. They own two businesses in town and Andrew enjoys piloting his own plane, family holidays and boating on the Gippsland Lakes. Following in his father's footsteps, he also enjoys adventures in his two Land Rovers. Since the sale of Jindi Cheese, Andrew has been heavily involved in politics and in 2014, was a member of the Victorian Legislative Council.

Jenny and her husband Glen also reside in Warragul with their son Jaziah (b.2003), and two daughters Mia (b.2005) and Indianna (b.2008). After spending many years as Youth Pastors at the Warragul Community Church, Glen is now a Chaplain/Teacher. Jenny owns and runs Treble's Music Studio in Warragul, teaching instrumental music. They both enjoy spending time with family and friends and touring the country in their caravan whenever they can. In 2013 Bev and I joined them travelling around Australia.

Narelle is married to Daniel with two children, Hannah (b.2007) and Ethan (b.2011). Narelle is a Business Analyst for an IT Company in Melbourne and Daniel is a Senior Manager in the building Industry. Narelle enjoys keeping fit and healthy and competing in triathlons while Daniel restores old cars in his man cave.

Shelley loves to travel, perhaps sparked by all those Jindi Cheese awards trips. She manages a Travel Agency in Melbourne and takes every opportunity to test the travel deals. Bev and I frequently use her services. Shelley met her husband Frederic while travelling the world and he is a foreman in a large motor company in Melbourne. Fortuitously, Fred shares my love of 4WDing.

All our children were raised in the house we built when we married in 1967 and we lived there until after the fires. Having been there all our married life, I really didn't want to move out of the home. The house looked down over the property and the Jindi factory. This was the same land I'd cleared and worked for so many years. Every day I awoke to see the property, business, and impressive garden we created together. It was right there. But after selling Jindi, we decided that we needed to move away from the factory. We had 66 acres of land which we bought in 1989. This was previously owned by my grandfather Oscar Ronalds which he purchased in 1895. This is where we built our present home and we moved a couple of weeks after the 2009 bush fires. The fires engulfing our garden and surrounds made the move somewhat easier. Selling Jindi enabled us to help many other people along the way and as a family to do many things that otherwise would not have been possible. It enabled us to enjoy very special holiday time travelling together with our children and grandchildren. What better harvest could a farmer hope for.

George and Bev Ronalds

Andrew, Catriona, Arabella and Madeline

Jaziah, Glen, Jenny, Mia and Indianna Treble

Hannah, Narelle, Daniel, Ethan Guglielmi

Shelley and Frederic Jacquemin

George playing with big toys at 80

www.ingramcontent.com/pod-product-compliance
Lightning Source LLC
Chambersburg PA
CBHW071849230426
43671CB00012B/2125